DATE DUE

GAYLORD

PRINTED IN U.S.

MODERN GENETICS

ENGINEERING LIFE

Lisa Yount

CHELSEA HOUSE
PUBLISHERS
An imprint of Infobase Publishing

To the memory of my parents, with thanks for a
lively set of genes, and to my brother, Stuart,
with whom I seem to share more of those genes
than either of us might have thought

MODERN GENETICS: Engineering Life
Copyright © 2006, 1997 by Lisa Yount

This is a revised edition of GENETICS AND GENETIC ENGINEERING
Copyright © 1997 by Lisa Yount

Chelsea House
An imprint of Infobase Publishing
132 West 31st Street
New York NY 10001

Library of Congress Cataloging-in-Publication Data

Yount, Lisa.
    Modern genetics: engineering life / Lisa Yount. — Rev. ed.
        p. cm.— (Milestone in discovery and invention)
    Includes bibliographical references and index.
    ISBN 0-8160-5744-3 (acid-free paper)
    1. Genetics—History—Juvenile literature. 2. Genetic engineering—History—
Juvenile literature. I. Yount, Lisa. Genetics and genetic engineering. II. Title.
III. Series.
    QH437.5Y68 2006
    576.5'09—dc22   2005018152

Chelsea House books are available at special discounts when purchased in bulk
quantities for businesses, associations, institutions, or sales promotions. Please call
our Special Sales Department in New York at (212) 967-8800 or (800) 322-8755.

You can find Chelsea House on the World Wide Web at
http://www.chelseahouse.com

Text design by James Scotto-Lavino
Cover design by Dorothy Preston
Illustrations by Lisa Goldfarb

Printed in the United States of America

MP FOF 10 9 8 7 6 5 4 3 2 1

This book is printed on acid-free paper.

CONTENTS

PREFACE

The Milestones in Science and Discovery set is based on a simple but powerful idea—that science and technology are not separate from people's daily lives. Rather, they are part of seeking to understand and reshape the world, an activity that virtually defines being human.

More than a million years ago, the ancestors of modern humans began to shape stones into tools that helped them compete with the specialized predators around them. Starting about 35,000 years ago, the modern type of human, *Homo sapiens,* also created elaborate cave paintings and finely crafted art objects, showing that technology had been joined with imagination and language to compose a new and vibrant world of culture. Humans were not only shaping their world but representing it in art and thinking about its nature and meaning.

Technology is a basic part of that culture. The mythologies of many peoples include a trickster figure, who upsets the settled order of things and brings forth new creative and destructive possibilities. In many myths, for instance, a trickster such as the Native Americans' Coyote or Raven steals fire from the gods and gives it to human beings. All technology, whether it harnesses fire, electricity, or the energy locked in the heart of atoms or genes, partakes of the double-edged gift of the trickster, providing power to both hurt and heal.

An inventor of technology is often inspired by the discoveries of scientists. Science as we know it today is younger than technology, dating back about 500 years to a period called the Renaissance. During the Renaissance, artists and thinkers began to explore nature systematically, and the first modern scientists, such as Leonardo da Vinci (1452–1519) and Galileo Galilei (1564–1642), used instruments and experiments to develop and test ideas about how objects in the universe behaved. A succession of revolutions followed, often introduced by individual geniuses: Isaac Newton (1643–1727) in mechanics and mathematics, Charles Darwin (1809–82) in biological evolution, Albert Einstein (1879–1955) in relativity and quantum physics, James Watson (1928–   ) and Francis Crick (1916–2004) in modern genetics. Today's emerging fields of science and technology, such as genetic engineering, nanotechnology, and artificial intelligence, have their own inspiring leaders.

The fact that particular names such as Newton, Darwin, and Einstein can be so easily associated with these revolutions suggests the importance of the individual in modern science and technology. Each book in this set thus focuses on the lives and achievements of eight to 10 individuals who together have revolutionized an aspect of science or technology. Each book presents a different field: marine science, genetics, astronomy and space science, forensic science, communications technology, robotics, artificial intelligence, and mathematical simulation. Although early pioneers are included where appropriate, the emphasis is generally on researchers who worked in the 20th century or are still working today.

The biographies in each volume are placed in an order that reflects the flow of the individuals' major achievements, but these life stories are often intertwined. The achievements of particular men and women cannot be understood without some knowledge of the times they lived in, the people they worked with, and developments that preceded their research. Newton famously remarked, "If I have seen further [than others], it is by standing on the shoulders of giants." Each scientist or inventor builds upon—or wrestles with—the work that has come before. Individual scientists and inventors also interact with others in their own laboratories and elsewhere, sometimes even partaking in vast collective efforts, such as the government and private projects that raced at the end of the 20th century to complete the description of the human genome. Scientists and inventors affect, and are affected by, economic, political, and social forces as well. The relationship between scientific and technical creativity and developments in social institutions is another important facet of this series.

A number of additional features provide further context for the biographies in these books. Each chapter includes a chronology and suggestions for further reading. In addition, a glossary and a general bibliography (including organizations and Web resources) appear at the end of each book. Several types of sidebars are also used in the text to explore particular aspects of the profiled scientists' and inventors' work:

Connections   Describes the relationship between the featured work and other scientific or technical developments.

I Was There   Presents firsthand accounts of discoveries or inventions.

Issues   Discusses scientific or ethical issues raised by the discovery or invention.

Other Scientists (or Inventors)   Describes other individuals who played an important part in the work being discussed.

Parallels   Shows parallel or related discoveries.

Social Impact   Suggests how the discovery or invention affects or might affect society and daily life.

Solving Problems   Explains how a scientist or inventor dealt with a particular technical problem or challenge.

Trends   Presents data or statistics showing how developments in a field changed over time.

Our hope is that readers will be intrigued and inspired by these stories of the human quest for understanding, exploration, and innovation. We have tried to provide the context and tools to enable readers to forge their own connections and to further pursue their fields of interest.

ACKNOWLEDGMENTS

Thanks to the scientists in this book who reviewed their chapters and answered questions, and to the many assistants of scientists who patiently conveyed messages and sent (and sometimes re-sent) photographs, permission forms, and other items. My thanks to my editor, Frank K. Darmstadt, as well for his help and good humor; to my cats, for providing purrs and not knocking the computer off my lap (though they tried); and, above all, to my husband, Harry Henderson, for unending support, love, and everything else that makes life good.

INTRODUCTION

"Any sufficiently advanced technology is indistinguishable from magic."
—*science fiction writer Arthur C. Clarke*

Most people love to watch magicians. These clever stage artists seem to make scarves or birds appear and then vanish again, "saw people in half" without really harming them, or escape from boxes covered with chains and padlocks. A magic show almost guarantees an entertaining evening.

Nonetheless, people have always had mixed feelings about magicians. Throughout history, they regarded men and women who called themselves magicians with both awe and suspicion. Was the "magic" merely a matter of illusions and tricks, or did it stem from some real, supernatural power? Would magicians make wishes and dreams come true, or would they cast evil spells that brought destruction? Concern about magicians' powers and motives was made greater by the fact that magicians almost never explained how they achieved their effects. Even when someone attempted an explanation, it was hard for most people to understand.

Many people today have the same mixed feelings about scientists and the technologists who build inventions upon science. They find scientists just as mysterious as magicians, and scientists' "tricks" seem just as hard to comprehend. Because of this, some people may let hopes and fears substitute for knowledge. Some believe that scientists and inventors will end hunger, provide clean and inexpensive energy, and solve a host of other problems. Others feel equally sure that those same scientists and inventors will produce massive environmental destruction or unstoppable epidemics. In both their hopes and their fears, much of today's public sees scientists and technologists as "playing God," just as magicians were once accused of doing.

No field of knowledge except nuclear physics, whose discoveries made possible the atomic bomb, has been as much of a lightning rod for people's hopes and fears about science as genetics and its technological offshoot, often called genetic engineering or biotechnology. Even more than most scientists, geneticists and genetic engineers—people who analyze and sometimes change the inherited information that controls the form and development of every living thing—seem to wield magic power.

Genetic Engineering Old and New

Many people think that genetics and genetic engineering are recent creations, and in a strict sense this is true. The scientific field of genetics is only a little more than 100 years old. Researchers have known what genes are, physically and chemically, for a mere 50 years, and they have been able to change genes directly for just half that time.

In other ways, however, the study of genetics, and even genetic engineering, is as old as humankind. People have always noticed that members of families tend to look alike, having similar hair or eye color, for instance. Sometimes parents and children share a certain trait or way of behaving, such as singing talent or a quick temper. Those qualities seem to have been passed down from one generation to the next. People who observed such similarities were seeing genetics in action.

Similarly, ancient farmers and herders realized that if they mated, or bred, plants or animals with desirable traits such as the ability to grow quickly or resist disease, they had a better than average chance of obtaining offspring with those same traits. People were also aware of characteristics such as strength and good health when they chose their own mates. In making decisions about mating and breeding, individuals were acting as unconscious genetic engineers.

Scientists began investigating inheritance of traits more systematically in the mid-19th century. In *On the Origin of Species*, published in 1859, British biologist Charles Darwin claimed that nature, in essence, behaved like plant and animal breeders. Characteristics of living things changed randomly over time, he wrote, but only the features that helped their possessors survive and reproduce continued to appear in generation after generation. Darwin's theory, which he called evolution by natural selection, caused great debate in his own time, but almost all scientists now accept it.

Only a few years later, Gregor Mendel (1822–84), an Austrian monk, offered the first precise explanation of how the traits Darwin wrote about might be transmitted. By breeding pea plants in his monastery garden, Mendel worked out rules that governed which form of traits such as height and seed color would be passed from parents to offspring.

Mendel's work, described in a paper published in 1866, was little known in his own time, but three European scientists independently rediscovered it at the start of the 20th century. Publicizing and building on Mendel's discoveries, these and other researchers of the time founded the branch of science that British biologist William Bateson (1861–1926) named genetics, which studies the way traits are inherited. Early geneticists chose the term *gene* for a unit of inheritance that conveys one trait, but no one knew what a gene actually was.

Thomas Hunt Morgan (1866–1945) and his coworkers at Columbia University performed breeding experiments on fruit flies in 1910 that proved that inherited information was carried on chromosomes. Pairs (23 pairs in humans) of these minute "colored bodies" exist in the nucleus, or central part, of cells. Chromosomes reproduce themselves just before a cell splits in two, so each new cell receives a full set. Morgan's group showed that a genetic change, or mutation, that produced an unusual eye color in the flies had to be carried on the same chromosome that determined a fly's gender, because the eye color mutation occurred only in males. Males had been shown to possess a chromosome called the Y chromosome, which females do not have.

Morgan's work told scientists where to look for genes. However, researchers still had no idea what substance in chromosomes contained genes or what chemical processes made genes able to reproduce and transmit information. They knew they could never really understand how genes worked until they learned these secrets. The search for the chemical nature of genes begins this book.

Fifty Years of Revolution

This volume in the Milestones in Discovery and Invention set tells the stories of 14 of the most famous geneticists and genetic engineers who worked during the 50 years between the discovery of the structure of DNA (deoxyribonucleic acid, the chemical that proved to carry the "code" for an organism's inherited traits) in 1953 and the final reading out of the human genome, humanity's complete collection of genes, in 2003. James Watson and Francis Crick in effect began the modern era of genetics by working out DNA's structure, which showed how DNA molecules could reproduce and encode inherited information. Building on this discovery, Crick and others in the 1960s deciphered the individual chemical "letters" that make up the DNA code and showed how the code is used to make proteins, the substances that carry out most activities in cells.

In 1973, Herbert Boyer and Stanley N. Cohen showed that scientists could change genes, not only indirectly through breeding but directly through biochemical manipulations. Boyer and Cohen also moved genetic material from one organism to another and showed that the material produced its normal proteins in its new location. In doing so, they invented what came to be called genetic engineering. Boyer also pioneered the use of genetic engineering in industry, cofounding Genentech, the first biotechnology company.

Unlike Watson and Crick's discovery, genetic engineering quickly attracted the attention of nonscientists as well as scientists. Writers such as Jeremy Rifkin, the president of the Foundation on Economic Trends, warned that this new technology might create microbes that would cause unstoppable epidemics or other dangerous life-forms. Many later genetic engineering projects also drew criticism from ethicists, religious leaders, politicians, and others.

A few years after Boyer and Cohen's achievement, Michael Bishop and Harold Varmus revealed the genetic underpinnings of cancer, one of humanity's most feared diseases. Genes able to produce cancer in animals had been found in viruses, but Bishop and Varmus showed in 1976 that the genes did not originate in these infectious microorganisms. Instead, cancer-causing genes were normal cellular genes gone awry. Other researchers later found several kinds of cancer-related genes in human tumors, opening up the possibility of developing drugs that would counteract the genes' activity.

French Anderson explored a more direct approach to controlling genetic problems: repairing or replacing the defective genes themselves. In 1991, Anderson and his coworkers inserted normal genes for producing a key immune system chemical into blood cells of a child who suffered a rare inherited illness caused by lack of this chemical. This treatment, the first gene therapy given to a human, restored the young girl to health. Meanwhile, Nancy Wexler and others tried to identify the mutated genes that produced inherited diseases such as Huntington's disease, a brain-destroying ailment that afflicted Wexler's family. Cooperative effort among several research groups led to identification of the Huntington's gene in 1993. In that same year, Cynthia Kenyon identified genes in worms that lengthened the worms' lifespan, hinting that genetic changes underlay not only inherited illnesses but the much more common diseases associated with aging.

Few people opposed changing genes to prevent or treat inherited illness, but some worried that the kind of gene alteration pioneered by French Anderson might eventually be used to eliminate normal human variation or create "designer babies" that would be more like purchased products than natural children. The work of Ian Wilmut, who announced in 1997 that he had cloned a sheep from a mature adult cell, and of James Thomson, who reported in 1998 that he had isolated cells from human embryos (unborn living things in a very early stage of development) that might be used to create any tissue in the body, aroused similar concern about the implications that these scientific advances might have for humanity. For many commentators, both men's research raised the frightening possibility that human beings might be cloned, even though neither scientist supported such an activity.

German-Swiss scientist Ingo Potrykus, whose laboratory used genetic engineering in 1998 to create rice containing a nutrient that many children in the developing world lack, encountered a different type of controversy. Potrykus said he wanted the rice to be a weapon against malnutrition, but critics claimed that agricultural biotechnology companies planned to use the rice as a tool to force genetically modified foods on an unwilling world.

Perhaps the loudest debates of all have arisen about the implications of the Human Genome Project, a massive undertaking to determine the complete genetic makeup of human beings. During the project's final years, media attention focused on the rivalry between Francis Collins, who led the international, government-sponsored project, and scientist-entrepreneur Craig Venter, who headed a private company that claimed it could complete the genome analysis sooner and more inexpensively than the government effort could. Once the project was complete, however, discussion centered on the ways the genome information might be used. Observers say that understanding the human genome could lead to greatly improved treatments for disease, unprecedented discrimination based on genetic makeup—or perhaps both.

Moving Away from Magic

Most scientists and inventors in the fields of genetics and genetic engineering welcome honest debate. They have usually thought hard about where their work might lead, and they expect others to do the same. Scientists and their supporters say, however, that before intelligent discussion can take place, people need to move beyond picturing these men and women as magicians, possessors of secret knowledge and godlike powers. Nonscientists must learn how the "gene magicians" perform their tricks and what their technology can and cannot accomplish. Only after gaining this knowledge, entering into the seeming magic themselves, will citizens be able to make thoughtful decisions about how the amazing power to understand and alter the basic blueprints of life should be used. I hope that this book will contribute to such education.

1

THE CODE OF LIFE

FRANCIS CRICK, JAMES WATSON, AND THE STRUCTURE OF DNA

Running a race—especially an Olympic-level race, in which the winner may become world famous—is anything but easy. The task would become immeasurably harder if the contestants had to run the race blindfolded. The scientists in the race to discover the structure of deoxyribonucleic acid (DNA) faced something like that challenge.

Only a few "runners" entered the competition. At the start of the 1950s, when the contest began, most potential entrants thought it was not worth their trouble. Researchers had known for decades that chromosomes, the tiny bodies in the cell nucleus that had been shown to carry inherited information (genes), were made of two kinds of complex chemicals: proteins and nucleic acids. One or the other of these groups of substances had to contain the information, coded somehow into the structure of their molecules. Most scientists who studied the subject thought that proteins would prove to be the gene carriers. Proteins, after all, are made up of 20 kinds of smaller molecules called amino acids, which allowed for numerous combinations within a protein molecule. Much less was known about nucleic acids, which Johann Miescher, a Swiss chemist, had discovered in 1869. However, biochemists had found that nucleic acids contain only four types of subunits, or bases. A chemical "alphabet" with four letters offered far fewer possibilities than one with 20. Most researchers therefore believed that finding out the exact structure of nucleic acid molecules was not important.

1

The easy comradeship of Francis Crick (left) and James Watson (right) helped them work out the structure of DNA at Britain's Cambridge University in 1953. (Image 6.1, James D. Watson Collection, Cold Spring Harbor Laboratory Archives)

A Mystery Molecule

A small number of molecular biologists, members of a relatively new scientific discipline that studies the structure and activities of molecules in living things, thought the protein supporters were wrong. They pointed to an experiment done in 1944 in which Oswald Avery, a researcher at New York's Rockefeller Institute, had mixed DNA from disease-causing bacteria with a living strain of related but harmless bacteria. After being exposed to the DNA, the harmless bacteria—and their descendants—became able to cause disease. This change strongly suggested that DNA, a nucleic acid, carried inheritable information that the harmless bacteria had somehow incorporated into their own genetic material.

The molecular biologists who had been convinced by Avery's experiment realized that in order to learn how DNA might reproduce itself and transmit inherited information, they needed to discover the structure of the DNA molecule. They would have to work "blindfolded," in the sense that earlier studies had provided very few clues to guide them.

The researchers knew that each DNA molecule contained many copies of the four types of bases, small molecules called adenine, cytosine, guanine, and thymine. The molecule also included at least one "backbone," a long string of identical, alternating sugar and phosphate molecules. X-ray crystallography, a technique that helped chemists analyze the shape of molecules, suggested that the backbone was shaped like a coil, or helix. Austrian-born biochemist Erwin Chargaff had shown in the late 1940s that the amount of cytosine in a DNA molecule was always the same as the amount of guanine, and the same was true of adenine and thymine. However, no one knew how many backbone strands each molecule of DNA contained or how the backbones and bases were arranged within the molecule.

The Race Begins

In 1951, three teams of molecular biologists, one in the United States and two in Britain, accepted their blindfolds and began the race to find the structure of DNA. Chemist Linus Pauling, at the California Institute of Technology (Caltech), led the U.S. group. Pauling had already become famous for working out the basic structure of protein molecules, which had also proved to be a helix.

One of the British groups was at King's College in London. Maurice Wilkins, a biophysicist from New Zealand, was its leader. British chemist Rosalind Franklin, an expert in X-ray crystallography, was among those who worked with him. Wilkins and Franklin, both brilliant scientists, did not get along with each other.

Just the opposite was true of the third team, a pair of researchers at Cambridge, one of Britain's two most famous universities. One of the duo was American, the other British. The United States scientist, James Dewey Watson, was the younger of the two. Born in Chicago on April 6, 1928, Watson entered the University of Chicago as part of a special program when he was only 15 years old. At first he planned to study birds, but by the time he obtained his B.S. in zoology in 1947, physicist Erwin Schrödinger's book *What Is Life?* had drawn his interest to genetics and the possibility that certain molecules might carry genetic information. Watson did graduate work on the genetics of viruses at Indiana University in Bloomington, receiving his Ph.D. in 1950.

While doing further study in Europe, Watson met Maurice Wilkins in spring 1951. Watson was already "obsessed," as he later put it, with DNA, and he believed that the DNA molecule's structure would hold the key to the way genes convey inherited information. When Wilkins told him that DNA could be studied by X-ray crystallography, Watson realized that this meant that DNA had regular, or repeated, features in its structure. *Current Biography Yearbook 1990* quotes Watson as saying he became convinced that the shape of a DNA molecule would be "simple as well as pretty."

In fall 1951, Watson, then 23 years old, joined the Cavendish Laboratory at Cambridge, where scientists were using X-ray crystallography to study protein molecules. There he met 35-year-old British scientist Francis Harry Compton Crick. Born on June 8, 1916, in Northampton, England, to a shoe manufacturer and his wife, Crick still did not have his Ph.D. at the time he met Watson. The British scientist had received a B.S. in physics from University College, London, in 1937, but World War II had interrupted his scientific career. When he began his schooling once more, he found his interests turning toward biology.

"I . . . immediately discovered the fun of talking to Francis Crick," Watson's *Current Biography* profile quotes him as saying. Crick, for his part, wrote in his autobiography, *What Mad Pursuit:*

Jim and I hit it off immediately, partly because our interests were astonishingly similar and partly, I suspect, because a certain youthful arrogance, a ruthlessness, and an impatience with sloppy thinking came naturally to both of us.

The most important interest the two men shared was in DNA. They were sure that discovering its structure would make them famous—if they could find the key to the puzzle before the King's College or the Caltech team did. Watson and Crick tried to solve their scientific problem mostly by thinking and talking. They also built models that showed possible molecular structures, just as Linus Pauling had done when working out the structure of proteins. The models let them see and manipulate possible structures for the DNA molecule in three dimensions.

The Winning Discovery

New Zealand–born biophysicist Maurice Wilkins led the laboratory at King's College, London, that competed with Watson and Crick in the race to discover the structure of DNA. (National Library of Medicine, photo B09719)

"In the process of [scientific] discovery," N. A. Tiley's book on key DNA research, *Discovering DNA*, quotes eminent modern science historian Horace Freeland Judson as saying, "there comes a unique moment: where great confusion reigned, the shape of an answer springs out—or at least the form of a question." Great confusion certainly reigned in the DNA race at the start of 1953. Watson and Crick had made a preliminary guess about DNA's structure in late 1952, but Rosalind Franklin had shown that they were wrong. Franklin, in turn, insisted that the molecule could not have the overall shape of a helix, which also proved to be a mistake. Finally, Linus Pauling announced in January 1953 that the DNA molecule contained three helix-shaped backbones. That conclusion was quickly shown to be incorrect as well.

For James Watson, the shape of the answer to the DNA puzzle began to appear on January 30, 1953, when he visited Maurice Wilkins at King's College. Even though the two men were rivals in the DNA race, they had become friends. During this visit, Wilkins showed Watson an X-ray photograph that Rosalind Franklin had made of DNA. As Watson looked at this picture, which was clearer than any others he had seen, "my mouth fell open and my pulse began to race," he wrote later in his memoir of the DNA discovery, *The Double Helix*. He realized that the DNA molecule most likely had two parallel, helix-shaped backbones.

Watson hurried back to Cambridge and described the photo to Crick. With the question of the backbones answered to their satisfaction, the pair turned their attention to the second major question: how the bases were arranged within the molecule. Crick concluded

---

SOLVING PROBLEMS: X-RAY CRYSTALLOGRAPHY

British physicist Lawrence Bragg invented X-ray crystallography in 1912. In this technique, a beam of X-rays is passed through a solid. Some of the rays bounce off atoms in the molecules within the solid, thereby changing the angles at which the rays strike a photographic plate on the other side of the solid. A photograph made from the plate shows a pattern of dark dots or smears on a light background. Interpreted by experts, photos of this kind reveal information about the three-dimensional placement of atoms within molecules—in other words, the molecules' structure.

At first, Bragg and his followers applied X-ray crystallography only to solids that had an orderly structure, which let the solids form crystals. In 1934, however, Desmond Bernal and W. T. Astbury, two other British scientists, showed how to use the technique to analyze substances with large, complex molecules that cannot form crystals, such as proteins and nucleic acids. Rosalind Franklin was a specialist in this new type of X-ray crystallography.

Franklin and other experts such as Dorothy Crowfoot Hodgkin used X-ray crystallography to work out the structure of many important biological molecules, including cholesterol and penicillin, during the late 1930s and 1940s. They became able to unravel even more complex substances in the 1950s, when computers took over the difficult mathematical calculations involved in interpreting the X-ray photographs.

that the bases must be inside the backbones, stretching between them like steps on a twisted ladder. At first, Watson thought the bases might appear as pairs of the same kind of molecule—adenine and adenine, for example. That did not fit what was known about the size of the space between the backbones, however.

Too impatient to wait for new metal models to be built, Watson cut model pieces from cardboard and began trying different arrangements. Two of the bases, adenine and guanine, were larger than the other two. Pairs of large bases were too big to fit between the intertwined backbones, and pairs of the smaller bases were too small. As Watson played with his cardboard cutouts, however, he noticed that a pair consisting of adenine, a large base, and thymine, a small one, had exactly the same size and shape as a pair made up of guanine and cytosine. Both types of pair fit nicely if placed horizontally between the two vertical backbones, just as Crick had suggested. A pairing of adenine with thymine and guanine with cytosine would also fit with Erwin Chargaff's finding about the proportions of bases in the DNA molecule. Bonds between the bases' hydrogen atoms could hold the pairs together, Watson believed.

As soon as Crick came into their shared office on the morning of February 28, Watson showed him the matching cardboard base pairs. Crick saw immediately that Watson's discovery meant that the sequence, or order, of the bases along the two backbones was complementary. If a person knew the sequence of bases attached to one backbone, the order of bases along the other could be predicted.

Watson and Crick wrote a short scientific paper that described their proposed structure. The paper appeared in the prestigious British science journal *Nature* on April 25, 1953. Only one understated sentence near the end of the report hinted at the discovery's importance: "It has not escaped our notice that the specific pairing we have postulated immediately suggests a possible copying mechanism for the genetic material."

How DNA Reproduces

On May 30, 1953, about five weeks after Watson and Crick's initial paper appeared, the two scientists published a second paper in *Nature* that explained the cryptic sentence in the first. If DNA carried hereditary information, Crick and Watson said, DNA molecules had to be able to reproduce themselves when chromosomes duplicated during cell division. The two men believed that the key to DNA's reproduction lay in the molecule's mirror-image structure. Just before a cell divides, they proposed, the weak hydrogen bonds between the pairs of bases in its DNA molecules break. Each molecule then splits lengthwise, like a zipper unzipping. Each base attracts its pair mate, complete with an attached backbone segment, from among free-floating materials in the cell nucleus. An adenine molecule always attracts a thymine and vice versa, and the same for

---

I WAS THERE: THE SECRET OF LIFE

In *The Double Helix,* James Watson described the moment when he told Francis Crick about his proposed structure for the DNA molecule on February 28, 1953:

> *Upon his arrival Francis did not get more than halfway through the door before I let loose that the answer to everything was in our hands. Though as a matter of principle he maintained skepticism for a few moments, the similarly shaped A-T and G-C pairs had their expected impact.*

Crick began experimenting with Watson's cardboard models himself and made several refinements to Watson's structure. Both men were soon convinced that they had essentially solved the DNA problem, although Watson remained cautious.

> *We both knew that we would not be home [completely sure their structure was right] until a complete model was built in which all the [features fitted with the X-ray data]. There was also the obvious fact that the implications of its existence were far too important to risk crying wolf. Thus I felt slightly queasy when at lunch Francis winged into the Eagle [a nearby bar] to tell everyone within hearing distance that we had found the secret of life.*

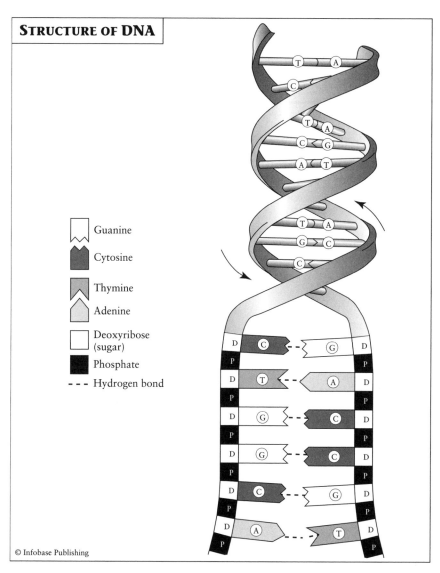

STRUCTURE OF DNA

Guanine
Cytosine
Thymine
Adenine
Deoxyribose (sugar)
Phosphate
- - - Hydrogen bond

© Infobase Publishing

James Watson and Francis Crick deduced in 1953 that each molecule of deoxy-
ribonucleic acid (DNA) is made up of two "backbones" composed of alternat-
ing smaller molecules of phosphate (P) and deoxyribose (D), a sugar. The back-
bones both have the shape of a helix, or coil, and they twine around each other.
Inside the backbones, like rungs on a ladder, are four kinds of smaller molecules
called bases. The bases always exist in pairs, connected by hydrogen bonds.
Adenine (A) always pairs with thymine (T), and cytosine (C) always pairs with
guanine (G).

cytosine and guanine. When the process is complete, the nucleus contains two identical double-stranded DNA molecules for every one that had existed before. The cell now splits, and each of the two daughter cells receives a complete copy of the original cell's DNA. Experiments later confirmed this theory.

Watson and Crick's discovery of DNA's structure earned them the Nobel Prize in physiology or medicine in 1962. Maurice Wilkins also shared in the prize. Rosalind Franklin could not, because she had died in 1958, and Nobel prizes are never awarded after a person's death. Numerous other awards, most given to Watson and Crick jointly, honored the same groundbreaking achievement, including the Albert Lasker Award for Basic Medical Research (1960), the Prix Charles Leopold Meyer from the French Academy of Sciences (1961), and the Research Corporation Award (1962). Watson also won the Medal of Freedom (1977) and the National Medal of Science (1997).

The Genetic Code

After his and James Watson's breakthrough discovery, Francis Crick continued to do research on DNA at Cambridge. (He received his Ph.D. from that institution in 1953.) He wanted to learn how a DNA molecule carries information and how it uses that information to make proteins, which other scientists had shown to be genes' chief task in the cell. The actions of proteins, in turn, create the traits that show themselves in living things.

Crick and Sydney Brenner, a fellow Cambridge scientist, proposed in 1955 that the sequence of bases in a DNA molecule acts as a code to determine the sequence of amino acids in protein molecules. Each "letter" of the code, the two researchers suggested, is a set of three bases arranged in a particular order. With four bases to work with, there could be 64 ($4 \times 4 \times 4$) such combinations, more than enough to represent all 20 amino acids.

Marshall Nirenberg of the National Institutes of Health and other molecular biologists set out to "crack" the DNA code in the early 1960s, determining by experiment which amino acid each set of three bases stood for. They learned that several different

REPLICATION OF DNA

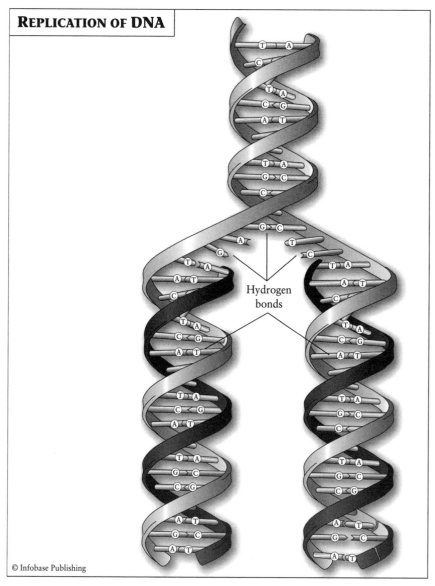

Hydrogen bonds

© Infobase Publishing

DNA's structure explains its power to duplicate itself. When a cell prepares to divide, the hydrogen bonds between the bases dissolve and the DNA molecule splits along its length like a zipper unzipping. Each half then attracts bases and backbone pieces from among the molecules in the cell, forming the same pairs of bases that had existed before. The result is two identical DNA molecules.

OTHER SCIENTISTS: ROSALIND FRANKLIN (1920–1958)

Rosalind Elsie Franklin was born on July 25, 1920, in London. Her well-to-do father at first discouraged her interest in science because he believed that higher education and careers made women unhappy. She persisted, however, and eventually studied chemistry at Newnham, a women's college in Cambridge University, graduating in 1941. Franklin did research on the structure of carbon molecules for the Coal Utilization Research Association during World War II and earned a Ph.D. from Cambridge on the basis of this work in 1945.

Franklin learned X-ray crystallography while doing research in France after the war. She became especially skilled at using the technique to study compounds that did not form crystals, which included most biological chemicals. This expertise brought her to Maurice Wilkins's laboratory at King's College, part of the University of London, in 1950. Wilkins hoped Franklin could take photographs that would help the group determine the structure of DNA molecules.

Some of Franklin's photographs were brilliant, and one of them helped James Watson and Francis Crick solve the puzzle of DNA's structure. (Wilkins has been criticized for showing this photograph to Watson without asking Franklin's permission first, but he felt that, as head of the laboratory, he had the right to do so.) Watson and others have said that Franklin herself might have worked out the DNA structure if she had had a scientific partner with whom she felt comfortable sharing her ideas.

Franklin left Wilkins's laboratory around the time Watson and Crick published their first DNA paper. She spent the rest of her all-too-short career studying the structure of viruses at Birkbeck, another college in the University of London.

Franklin died of ovarian cancer in 1958, when she was only 38 years old, leaving forever unsettled the question of whether she would have shared in the 1962 Nobel Prize given to Watson, Crick, and Wilkins. According to Franklin biographer Anne Sayre, J. D. Bernal, the X-ray crystallography expert under whom Franklin worked at Birkbeck, said of her, "As a scientist Miss Franklin was distinguished by extreme clarity and perfection in everything she undertook. Her photographs are among the most beautiful X-ray photographs . . . ever taken."

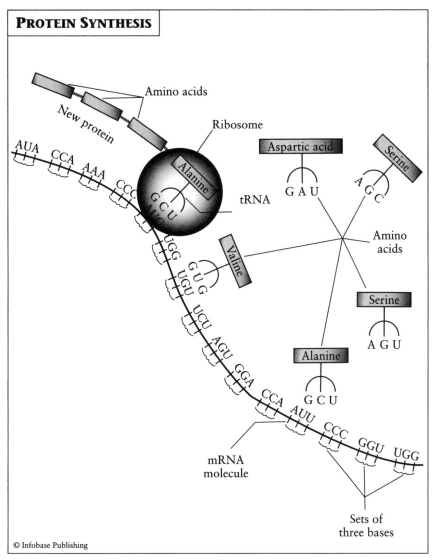

PROTEIN SYNTHESIS

Amino acids

New protein

Ribosome

AUA
CCA
AAA
CCC
AUC

Alanine
G C U

tRNA

Aspartic acid

G A U

Serine

A G C

Amino acids

Serine

A G U

Valine
G U G
UGU

UGG
UCU
AGU
GGA
CCA
AUU
CCC
GGU
UGG

Alanine
G C U

mRNA molecule

Sets of three bases

© Infobase Publishing

As a first step in making a protein, part of a DNA molecule (a gene) uses itself as a pattern to form a matching stretch of messenger RNA (mRNA). When the messenger RNA moves into the cytoplasm of the cell, it attracts matching short stretches of transfer RNA (tRNA), each of which tows a single amino acid molecule. With the help of an organelle called a ribosome, the transfer RNA molecules lock onto the matching parts of the messenger RNA, and the amino acids they carry are joined, forming a protein.

base triplets often stood for the same amino acid. Some additional groups marked the beginning or end of a gene. (Each DNA molecule contains hundreds or even thousands of genes.) By 1965, researchers had a "dictionary" that included all 64 three-base combinations.

While the details of the code were being worked out, Crick, Brenner, and others were learning the mechanism by which DNA uses its code to make proteins. Crick and Brenner suggested that DNA makes a copy of itself in the form of RNA (ribonucleic acid), which is like DNA except that it has a different kind of sugar in its backbones, and in place of thymine it has a different base, uracil. DNA normally cannot leave a cell's nucleus, but its RNA copy, which came to be called messenger RNA, can travel into the cytoplasm, the jellylike material that makes up the outer part of the cell.

In the cytoplasm, Crick and Brenner said, the messenger RNA encounters small bodies called ribosomes. A ribosome rolls along the messenger RNA molecule and attracts from the cytoplasm the amino acid represented by each three-base "letter" of the translated DNA code. Crick believed that what he called adapter molecules (later called transfer RNA) tow the amino acids to the correct spots on the messenger RNA. The amino acids then join together, forming the protein. The messenger RNA and the ribosome release the protein molecule into the cell. Brenner and other researchers in the early 1960s proved that this theory was essentially correct.

Diverging Careers

Francis Crick remained a researcher all his life. From the mid-1960s to the mid-1970s he studied the way animals develop before birth. In 1977, he moved to the Salk Institute for Biological Studies in La Jolla, California, and began to focus on the brain. Working mostly at a theoretical level, he investigated the way mammals' brains interpret visual data and process information during dreaming. He also wrote books on various subjects, including the possible origin of life and the nature of consciousness. Crick died of cancer on July 28, 2004.

James Watson, by contrast, eventually exchanged laboratory work for teaching and administration. He returned to the United

States soon after his famous discovery. He spent most of the next 15 years researching the structure of RNA and, like Crick (although independently of his former partner), the part that this nucleic acid played in the making of proteins. Beginning in 1956, Watson also taught at Harvard University.

Watson became director of Cold Spring Harbor Laboratory (CSHL) on Long Island, New York, in 1968. He left Harvard in 1976 to work at CSHL full time. He modernized this famous laboratory, the first genetics laboratory established in the United States, and focused its research on the biology of cancer, which was proving to be intimately related to genetics. Watson was president of CSHL from 1994 to 2003, after which he became the institution's chancellor.

Watson also found that he had literary skills. His memoir of the DNA race, *The Double Helix,* became a best seller when it was published in 1968. Some critics complained about his harsh portraits of other scientists, especially Rosalind Franklin, but readers enjoyed his breezy writing style and the book's behind-the-scenes picture of scientists at work. According to a 2004 *Chicago Tribune* article by William Mullen, Watson says he is more proud of this book than of his codiscovery of DNA's structure. "The DNA structure was going to be found within two or three years, anyway," Watson claimed. "But my book was my creation, something nobody else could have done." Watson later wrote many other books, including a second volume of autobiography and a highly regarded textbook on the molecular biology of genes.

In 1989, when Watson was 60 years old, the U.S. government chose him to direct the newest and biggest genetic project of all: the international Human Genome Project, sometimes called "biology's moon shot." Watson resigned this position in 1992, but he remains a strong supporter of the genome project and of genetic research in general.

The Companion to the History of Modern Science quotes Horace Freeland Judson as saying that "biology has proceeded by 'openings up'" rather than through the complete changes of world view that often occurred in physics. James Watson and Francis Crick's discovery of the structure of DNA sparked one of the biggest "openings up" of all. Nobel-winning scientist and science historian Peter Medawar, quoted in Dennis L. Breo's article about Watson and Crick's achievement in the *Journal of the American Medical Association* (February

24, 1993), said that the unraveling of the structure of DNA and the later discoveries built on it make up "the greatest achievement of science in the 20th century."

Chronology

1869	Johann Miescher discovers nucleic acids
1912	British physicist Lawrence Bragg invents X-ray crystallography
1916	Francis Crick born on June 8 in Northampton, England
1928	James Watson born on April 6 in Chicago, Illinois
1944	Oswald Avery shows that bacteria's inherited traits can be changed by exposing them to pure DNA
1940s	Late in the decade, Erwin Chargaff shows relationship among quantities of bases in DNA
1950	Watson obtains Ph.D. from University of Indiana, Bloomington
1951	Watson meets Maurice Wilkins in the spring and learns that the DNA molecule has repeating features in its structure
	Watson and Crick meet at Cambridge University in England in the fall
1952	Watson and Crick make a tentative proposal about DNA's structure late in the year; Rosalind Franklin proves them wrong
	Franklin insists that the DNA molecule cannot be a helix
1953	Linus Pauling proposes an incorrect structure for DNA in January
	On January 30, Maurice Wilkins shows Watson an X-ray photograph of DNA made by Rosalind Franklin
	Watson and Crick work out the structure of the DNA molecule on February 28
	On April 25, *Nature* publishes Watson and Crick's paper describing their proposed structure of the DNA molecule

On May 30, *Nature* publishes a second paper, in which Watson and Crick propose a mechanism by which a DNA molecule could make a copy of itself

Late in the year, Crick receives his Ph.D. from Caius College, Cambridge

1955 Crick and Sydney Brenner propose that the sequence of bases in DNA is the code by which the molecule orders the assembly of proteins and that each "letter" of the code consists of three bases in a certain order

Crick and Brenner suggest a mechanism by which DNA arranges the making of proteins through use of an intermediate molecule, RNA

1956 Watson joins faculty of Harvard University

1958 Rosalind Franklin dies of ovarian cancer

1961–1965 Marshall Nirenberg and others decipher the genetic code

Sydney Brenner and others verify the process by which DNA makes proteins

1962 Watson, Crick, and Maurice Wilkins win Nobel Prize for their discovery of structure of DNA

1968 Watson becomes director of Cold Spring Harbor Laboratory

Watson's memoir of his DNA discovery, *The Double Helix,* is published and becomes a best seller

1976 Watson leaves Harvard to work at Cold Spring Harbor Laboratory full time

1977 Crick moves to Salk Institute for Biological Studies in La Jolla, California, and begins theoretical studies of the brain

1989 Watson named first director of Human Genome Project

1992 Watson resigns as head of Human Genome Project

1994 Watson becomes president of Cold Spring Harbor Laboratory

2003 Watson steps down as president of Cold Spring Harbor Laboratory and becomes the institution's chancellor

2004 Francis Crick dies on July 28

Further Reading

Books

Crick, Francis. *What Mad Pursuit.* New York: Basic Books, 1988.
    Crick's autobiography, including his recollections about the discovery
    of DNA's structure.
Edelson, Edward. *Francis Crick and James Watson and the Building
    Blocks of Life.* New York: Oxford University Press, 1998.
    Account of the famous discovery, written for high school students.
Friedberg, Errol C. *The Writing Life of James D. Watson.* Cold
    Spring Harbor, N.Y.: Cold Spring Harbor Laboratory, 2004.
    Surveys Watson's books and essays.
Judson, Horace Freeland. *The Eighth Day of Creation.* New York:
    Simon and Schuster, 1979.
    Describes Watson and Crick's discovery of DNA's structure and other
    key discoveries in genetics and molecular biology from the mid-1930s
    to about 1970.
Olby, R. C., et al., eds. *Companion to the History of Modern Science.*
    London: Routledge, 1990.
    Essays describe different aspects of the history of science.
Sayre, Anne. *Rosalind Franklin and DNA.* New York: W. W. Norton,
    1975.
    Biography strongly sympathetic to Franklin provides a view of the
    DNA race that contrasts to Watson's.
Tiley, N. A. *Discovering DNA.* New York: Van Nostrand Reinhold,
    1983.
    Describes Watson and Crick's and other discoveries about DNA in the
    mid-20th century.
Watson, James D. *The Double Helix.* New York: Atheneum, 1968.
    Lively but biased memoir about the discovery of the structure of DNA.

Articles

Breo, Dennis L. "The Double Helix—Watson and Crick's 'Freak
    Find' of How Like Begets Like," *Journal of the American Medical
    Association* 269 (February 24, 1993): 1,040–1,045.
    Recalls how Watson and Crick made their discovery 40 years previ-
    ously.

"Crick, Francis (Harry Compton)." *Current Biography Yearbook 1983, 68–71.* New York: H. W. Wilson, 1983.
Profile of Crick summarizes other material written about him up to that time.
Mullen, William. "Genetic Pioneer James Watson Recalls a Chicago Education." *Chicago Tribune,* 4 February 2004, n.p.
Describes Watson's Chicago roots and later achievements.
Watson, J. D., and F. H. C. Crick. "Genetical Implications of the Structure of Deoxyribonucleic Acid," *Nature,* 30 May 1953, pp. 964–967.
Scientific paper describing how DNA's structure could allow it to reproduce itself.
———. "Molecular Structure of Nucleic Acids: A Structure for Deoxyribose Nucleic Acid," *Nature,* 25 April 1953, pp. 737–738.
The short scientific paper in which Watson and Crick propose a structure for the DNA molecule.
"Watson, James (Dewey)." *Current Biography Yearbook 1990,* 605–607. New York: H. W. Wilson, 1990.
Biographical article about Watson includes quotes from several interviews.

Web Sites

Access Excellence. This site for health and bioscience teachers and learners, sponsored by the National Health Museum, includes biographical profiles of Francis Crick and James Watson, interviews with them, and an account of their discovery of DNA's structure. www.accessexcellence.org. Accessed on December 29, 2004.

GENE SANDWICHES TO GO

HERBERT BOYER, STANLEY N. COHEN, AND THE BIRTH OF GENETIC ENGINEERING

It seems fitting that genetic engineering, in a sense, started in a delicatessen. Like the server behind the counter in a deli, genetic engineers can slice genes to order, sandwich them together with genes from other living things, and wrap up the package "to go." In doing so, they create completely new kinds of organisms. Both supporters and critics of genetic engineering agree that this technology opens up possibilities that will greatly affect science, human society, and perhaps all life on Earth.

A Chat over Corned Beef

The deli where genetic engineering was born is in Honolulu, Hawaii. Molecular biologists Stanley Norman Cohen of Stanford University and Herbert Wayne Boyer of the University of California, San Francisco (UCSF), dropped into the eatery one evening in November 1972, following a long day of meetings at a scientific conference.

Cohen, born in Perth Amboy, New Jersey, on February 17, 1935, had heard a speech that Boyer gave that day, and he was eager to learn more about the work the UCSF researcher was doing. When Cohen began to talk about his own research, Boyer became equally interested. As they devoured their pastrami and corned beef sandwiches, the two men came to realize that their areas of expertise fitted together as neatly as the pairs of bases in a DNA molecule. By joining forces, they thought they might be able to do something truly remarkable.

A husky former high school football star from Derry, Pennsylvania, Boyer was a year and a half younger than Cohen, having been born on July 10, 1936. Boyer had studied biology and chemistry at St. Vincent College in Pennsylvania, obtaining a bachelor's degree in 1958. He earned his master's degree in 1960 and his Ph.D. in 1963 from the University of Pittsburgh. After doing postgraduate work at Yale University, Boyer joined the UCSF faculty in 1966 as an assistant professor.

As Boyer explained to Cohen in the delicatessen, he was currently

During a conversation in a Hawaiian delicatessen, Stanley N. Cohen of Stanford University helped plan the experiments that led to genetic engineering. (Stanford University)

working with restriction enzymes, chemicals that certain bacteria make. These "molecular scissors" slice through strands of DNA wherever they find a particular sequence of bases. The bacteria use the enzymes to cut invading viruses apart before the viruses can reproduce and kill the bacteria. Boyer believed that the enzymes offered a way to divide immensely long DNA molecules into manageable—and predictable—chunks. Different restriction enzymes cut DNA at different sequences, so molecular biologists could choose how they would slice their DNA by deciding which enzyme to use.

One of the most interesting things about restriction enzymes, Boyer told Cohen, was that these "scissors" were not very sharp. Instead of cutting cleanly through a DNA molecule, they left an incomplete sequence of bases dangling from each end of the cut piece. Just as happened when DNA reproduced, these dangling bases were strongly attracted to other bases that would complete their usual pairings. That meant that the sequence from one snipped piece of DNA would attach easily to the opposite end of another piece of DNA that had been cut by the same enzyme, even if the two DNA fragments came from different kinds of living things. Other enzymes called ligases could then be used to glue the "sticky ends" together.

Cohen, whose background included a bachelor's degree from Rutgers University (1956) and an M.D. from the University of Pennsylvania School of Medicine (1960), had come to Stanford in 1968. He told Boyer that his own work with bacteria involved some unusual features of the microorganisms' genetics. In 1965, he said, scientists had discovered that, in addition to the large, ring-shaped DNA molecule that carries most of the bacteria's genetic information, bacteria often contain smaller rings of DNA called plasmids. Each plasmid holds only a few genes. When a bacterium reproduces itself by splitting in half, it reproduces not only its main genome but any plasmids it contains as well.

Bacteria do not exchange genes through sex, as many living things do. However, they sometimes exchange plasmids during a process called conjugation. In 1971, Cohen had found a way to imitate conjugation, removing plasmids from bacterial cells and making other bacteria take up the DNA pieces. He hoped to use this technique to help other scientists analyze individual genes or segments of DNA. Such analysis required millions of identical copies of a gene. Bacteria multiply at amazing speed, doubling their number every 20 minutes, so a single bacterium can produce millions more like itself in a single day. Cohen hoped that if he could find a way to insert a gene into the DNA of plasmids and then put the plasmids into bacteria, the bacteria would copy, or clone, the added gene as they reproduced. Boyer's enzymes, Cohen now realized with mounting excitement, might offer just the tools he needed to break open the rings of plasmid DNA, add the genes he wanted to copy, and reseal the plasmids.

The First Gene Splicing

By the time Boyer and Cohen had finished their sandwiches, the two researchers had planned a series of experiments that would combine

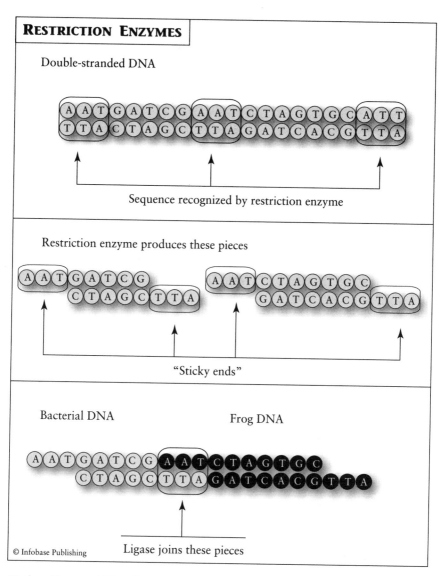

Herbert Boyer told Stanley Cohen that restriction enzymes, made by bacteria, could cut DNA molecules at certain sequences, leaving short pieces of single-stranded DNA at both ends of each segment. Each single-stranded piece can "stick to" any other single-stranded DNA piece containing a complementary sequence of bases. Cohen and Boyer realized that this fact might allow them to combine segments of DNA from different species.

their knowledge. In spring 1973, after they returned to California, they began carrying out those experiments. With the help of coworkers Annie Chang and Robert Helling, the two first used one of Boyer's restriction enzymes to cut open some of Cohen's plasmids. As Cohen had hoped, the "sticky ends" left by the inefficient molecular scissors let them join two different plasmids together to make a single large one. Cohen called the new plasmid a chimera, after a monster from ancient Greek legend that was part lion, part goat, and part snake.

The plasmids used in Cohen and Boyer's first experiment came from two different strains of *Escherichia coli,* a common and usually harmless bacterium that lives in the human intestine. One plasmid carried a gene that made the bacteria resistant to the antibiotic tetracycline, while the other had a gene that produced resistance to kanamycin, a different antibiotic. Boyer and Cohen put the altered plasmids into bacteria that normally would be killed by both types of drug, and then transferred the bacteria to a culture dish containing the two antibiotics. Some of the bacteria survived, showing that both of their newly acquired resistance genes were making proteins. For the first time, human beings had moved genes from one type of living thing to another and proved that the genes could function afterward.

In a second experiment, Boyer and Cohen combined plasmids from two different species of bacteria. A third test went still further, putting a gene from a frog into a plasmid. In both cases, the new plasmids functioned when put into bacteria, and they were copied when the bacteria multiplied. The bacteria containing these plasmids were essentially new kinds of organisms.

Cohen called his and Boyer's new technique "recombinant DNA." It later became known colloquially as gene splicing. Although a 2004 *Genomics and Genetics Weekly* article quotes Cohen as saying, "Herb and I didn't set out to invent genetic engineering. We set out to study basic biological phenomena," other molecular biologists were quick to realize the potential value of the pair's research. After hearing Boyer describe the work at a scientific meeting in 1973, according to Edwin Shorter's book on the development of the National Institutes of Health, *The Health Century,* one scientist summed up everyone's reaction by saying, "Well, now we can put together any DNA we want to."

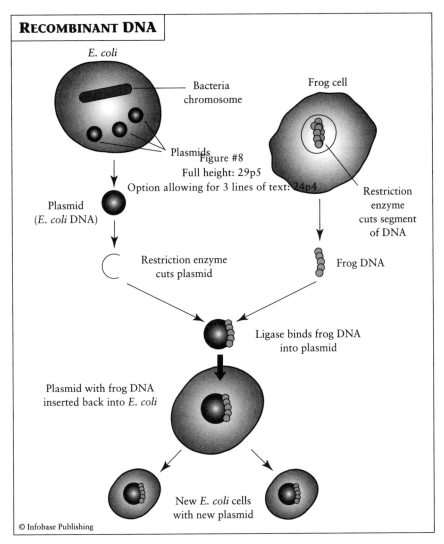

RECOMBINANT DNA

E. coli

Bacteria chromosome

Frog cell

Plasmids

Figure #8
Full height: 29p5
Option allowing for 3 lines of text: 24p4

Plasmid
(E. coli DNA)

Restriction enzyme cuts segment of DNA

Restriction enzyme cuts plasmid

Frog DNA

Ligase binds frog DNA into plasmid

Plasmid with frog DNA inserted back into E. coli

New E. coli cells with new plasmid

© Infobase Publishing

In one of their groundbreaking gene-splicing experiments, Stanley Cohen and Herbert Boyer broke up cells of a common bacterium, E. coli, and took out small, ring-shaped pieces of DNA called plasmids. They then used a restriction enzyme to cut the plasmids open. They used the same enzyme to produce segments of DNA from the cells of frogs. The bacterial and frog DNA segments joined together because of the complementary "sticky ends" of single-stranded DNA attached to each segment. Boyer and Cohen used a ligase, another type of enzyme, to bind the segments together, creating a new plasmid that contained frog as well as bacterial DNA. The researchers then inserted the plasmids carrying the foreign genes into other E. coli bacteria and showed that the foreign genes could make their normal proteins. When the bacteria multiplied, the added genes were duplicated along with the bacteria's own genetic material.

Is Genetic Engineering Dangerous?

Two floors above Cohen's laboratory at Stanford was the laboratory of another molecular biologist, Paul Berg. Berg might have created genetically engineered organisms before Cohen and Boyer—if concern about the possible results of his experiments had not stopped him.

A few months before Boyer and Cohen's experiments began, Berg removed a gene from SV40, a type of virus that infects monkeys, and combined it with the genome of another virus called lambda, which attacks bacteria. Lacking Boyer's restriction enzymes, he painstakingly attached "sticky" pieces of single-stranded DNA to the ends of his virus genes by chemical means. He then joined the genetic pieces with a ligase. Berg thus became the first person to combine genes from two different types of living things. He did not put the genes into an organism or prove that they could still function, however.

Berg had planned to use lambda as a vector, or carrier, to insert SV40 genes into *E. coli*. When Robert Pollack, a geneticist working at Cold Spring Harbor Laboratory in Long Island, New York, heard about this proposed experiment, however, he phoned Berg in alarm. SV40 was harmless in monkeys, Pollack pointed out, but it caused cancer in mice and hamsters. Pollack was worried about the possible dangers of inserting genes from a cancer-causing virus into a bacterium that could live inside the human body.

Berg decided that it would be wise to heed Pollack's warning, and he called off his experiments. When he heard about the work being done by Boyer, Cohen, and others, he became concerned about the safety of some of their projects as well.

Setting Standards

Late in 1973, Berg and 77 other molecular biologists sent a letter to the prestigious American scientific journal *Science*. It asked the U.S. National Academy of Sciences to look into possible dangers of recombinant DNA research and establish safety guidelines for experiments in this new field.

OTHER SCIENTISTS: PAUL BERG (1926–   )

Born on June 30, 1926, in Brooklyn, New York, Paul Berg was the son of a clothing manufacturer. His study of biochemistry at Pennsylvania State College was interrupted by World War II, in which he fought in the navy. He finally obtained his bachelor's degree in 1948. He earned a Ph.D. in biochemistry from Western Reserve University, now Case Western Reserve, in Cleveland, Ohio, in 1952. Before he came to Stanford in 1959, he taught at the Washington University School of Medicine in St. Louis.

Berg's first major research achievement, made in 1956, proved part of Francis Crick and Sydney Brenner's theory about how proteins were made. Crick and Brenner had suggested a year earlier that small molecules that they called adapter molecules towed individual amino acids into place and attached them to growing protein molecules. Berg found the first type of adapter molecule (transfer RNA) to be identified and showed that it always attached itself to an amino acid called methionine.

The work Berg was doing in 1972 and 1973 also grew out of discoveries by Watson and Crick. After the two scientists worked out the structure of DNA, they proposed that the double-stranded DNA molecule would reproduce by splitting apart. Each of the resulting single strands would then rebuild its partner strand by attracting free-floating bases in the cell. Berg demonstrated that short single strands of DNA did stick to other strands containing a complementary sequence of bases. For instance, a strand with the sequence C-A-A-T-G would bond to one with the sequence G-T-T-A-C.

Berg's planned experiment of combining virus genes and trying to make the altered viruses put the combined genes into bacteria was a first step toward introducing new genes into cells from mammals, James Watson (with Andrew Berry) writes in *DNA: The Secret of Life,* his history of DNA research. Eventually, Watson says, Berg hoped to use viruses to carry healthy genes into the cells of people with genetic diseases. Almost two decades later, French Anderson and others employed this same idea in developing gene therapy.

Berg won a share of the Nobel Prize in chemistry in 1980 for his pioneering work on the biochemistry of genes. He has also received other awards, including the Albert Lasker Award for basic medical research (1980) and the National Medal of Science (1985).

The scientists' call for caution went still further in a second letter, published in July 1974. Berg, Boyer, Cohen, and the other signers of the letter asked other researchers in the field to agree to a moratorium, or temporary halt, for some kinds of gene-altering research until the possible hazards of such work had been evaluated and more adequate safety precautions had been developed. The scientists were afraid that bacteria with dangerous added traits, such as the power to cause cancer or resist antibiotics, might escape from genetic engineers' laboratories and infect humans.

These safety fears resulted in a groundbreaking meeting of 140 molecular biologists at Asilomar, a retreat center in central California,

---

ISSUES: CONTINUING SAFETY CONCERNS

Most experts now think that the chances of a dangerous genetically modified microorganism escaping a laboratory on its own are small. Especially after the al-Qaeda attacks of September 2001, however, fear has grown that terrorists might create and release such deadly microbes deliberately. Defectors from Soviet biological warfare laboratories reported in the 1990s that the laboratories had conducted genetic engineering experiments on disease-causing bacteria, for instance.

Two experiments in the early 2000s were innocent in themselves, but they showed how easy creating a deadly microorganism could be. In the first experiment, described in February 2001, Australian scientists genetically altered the virus that causes mousepox, a disease similar to the often fatal human disease smallpox, and thereby accidentally made a virus that could kill mice vaccinated against the standard form of mousepox. Secondly, scientists at the State University of New York at Stony Brook reported in July 2002 that they had used information available on the Internet and DNA purchased through the mail to create "from scratch" a virus capable of causing the crippling disease polio. Members of Congress and even some scientists questioned whether accounts of research of this kind should be published, saying that terrorists might read them and put the methods described in the reports to terrible use.

in February 24–27, 1975. The meeting was also spurred by a second concern: the possibility that if scientists did not establish rules for this new technology, legislators would. Alarming stories about genetic engineering were beginning to appear in newspapers, radio, and television, and the public was demanding that the technology be controlled.

By the end of their argumentative meeting, the Asilomar group had devised guidelines for conducting different types of gene-splicing experiments. The National Institutes of Health (NIH), the chief research institutions sponsored by the U.S. government, used the Asilomar guidelines as a model when it drew up its own safety rules in 1976. The NIH rules were binding on all scientists receiving funding from the federal government, and most other U.S. researchers,

Herbert Boyer not only co-developed genetic engineering but helped found the modern biotechnology industry. (Albert and Mary Lasker Foundation)

especially those at universities, agreed to follow them as well. The NIH also established the Recombinant DNA Advisory Committee (RAC) to review future genetic engineering experiments.

These government steps quieted public fears. After several years of gene-splicing experiments passed without major problems, most of the NIH rules were dropped in 1980. The RAC, however, remains in existence. Its main job is to review experiments or drug tests in which altered genes are transferred into humans (gene therapy).

Bacterial Bonanzas

Even while scientific and public fear of gene splicing was at its height, excitement about the new technology's promise was equally strong.

Many people hoped that genetic engineering would produce new ways to treat disease or increase the world's food supply. In addition, farsighted businesspeople began to suspect that gene alteration might help them make a great deal of money.

Herbert Boyer was one of the first scientists to grasp this idea. Early in 1976, Robert Swanson, a 27-year-old venture capitalist, persuaded Boyer to join him in starting a business that would use genetic engineering techniques. The two men called their company Genentech, for GENetic ENgineering TECHnology.

Genentech, like similar companies formed soon afterward by other scientists and entrepreneurs, drew on Boyer and Cohen's discovery that foreign genes put into bacteria could produce the proteins that the genes had made in their original location, even if the bacteria normally would never make those proteins. As the bacteria and their added genes multiplied, the bacterial colonies in effect became tiny factories that potentially could churn out desirable proteins in tremendous amounts.

A Winning Product

The first commercial product that Genentech made in its bacterial factories was insulin, a protein that controls the way the body uses sugar. Insulin is normally made by certain cells in the pancreas, an organ in the abdomen that helps with digestion. Damage to these cells results in an illness called diabetes. People with diabetes will die unless they take insulin, usually in the form of daily injections.

Insulin can be extracted in relatively large amounts from the pancreases of slaughtered cattle and pigs, so diabetics could obtain this vital drug fairly cheaply even before genetic engineering. Pig and cow insulin, however, are not exactly the same as human insulin, and about 5 percent of people with diabetes are allergic to these animal substances. Bacteria containing the gene that produces human insulin make a substance essentially identical to the human form of the compound. Even though the percentage of diabetics who were allergic was small, 5 percent of the 8 million diabetics in the United States amounted to enough potential customers that Boyer and Swanson believed they could make a profit. Besides, they reasoned,

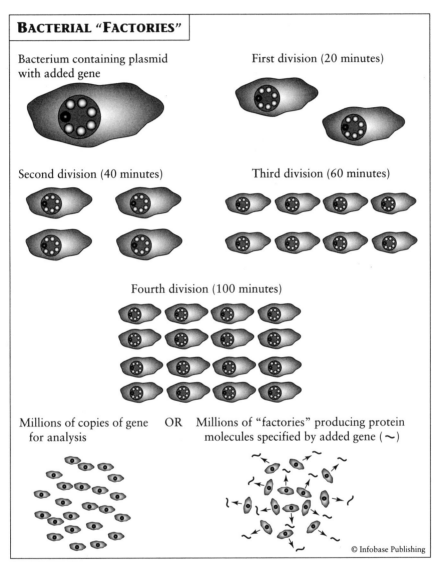

BACTERIAL "FACTORIES"

Bacterium containing plasmid with added gene

First division (20 minutes)

Second division (40 minutes)

Third division (60 minutes)

Fourth division (100 minutes)

Millions of copies of gene for analysis   OR   Millions of "factories" producing protein molecules specified by added gene (∼)

© Infobase Publishing

Bacteria can reproduce (by dividing) as often as once every 20 minutes. If genes from other organisms have been added to the bacteria, these genes will be copied along with the bacteria's own each time the microorganisms divide. In laboratory science, genetically engineered bacteria can be used to produce the millions of copies (clones) of a DNA fragment needed to analyze the base sequence in the fragment. In the biotechnology industry, the engineered bacteria act as miniature "factories" to produce proteins specified by their added genes.

I WAS THERE: THE FOUNDING OF GENENTECH

Herbert Boyer seemed to like casual locations for important conversations. The talk with Stanley Cohen that produced the pair's famous experiments in genetic engineering took place in a delicatessen, and the chat with Robert Swanson that led to the founding of Genentech happened in a bar.

In a series of interviews with Sally Smith Hughes in 1994, done as part of oral history programs conducted by the University of California at San Francisco and Berkeley, Boyer recalled the meeting with Swenson. It began in his laboratory, he said; the bar came later.

> He [Swanson] said he took a list of names associated with the publicity on Asilomar and went through it alphabetically, which means Paul Berg must have turned him down. I suppose I was next on the list. It was a telephone introduction. He wanted to talk, so I had him come to my lab on a Friday afternoon at quarter to five. He introduced himself, talked about what he wanted to do. . . . We spent a good deal of time that evening talking about it.

Boyer had no idea how to start a company. Swanson, however, offered to provide business expertise as well as money for the venture. Boyer was ready to listen. Perhaps lifting a beer mug in salute, as a sculpture in front of Genentech's San Francisco headquarters shows, Boyer (he told Hughes) said, "Sure, why not."

if their technique could produce one protein used in medicine, it could probably produce others equally well.

Genentech produced its first genetically engineered human insulin in 1978, winning a close race with several other companies that were pursuing the same goal. By September 1980, when Genentech first offered its stock to the public, the federal Food and Drug Administration (FDA) had not yet approved the new form of insulin for sale, as it must do with all new medicines. Nonetheless, investors' excitement about the new technology was so great that the price of the stock rose from $35 to $89 per share in the first few minutes of trading. James Watson writes in his history of DNA research, *DNA: The Secret of Life,* "At the time, this was the most rapid escalation in value in the history of Wall Street." Genentech began selling recombinant human insulin through Eli Lilly, a huge drug company, when the FDA granted approval in 1982.

Genetic engineers' menu of "gene sandwiches" has grown longer each year since then. The list came to include human growth hormone, given to people who would otherwise remain very short because they lack the hormone, and tPA, a drug that helps dissolve blood clots after heart attacks. Vaccines that protect people against diseases such as hepatitis B, a serious liver disease that can lead to cancer, have also been made by genetic engineering. Genentech itself continues to make successful products, including an anticancer drug called Avastin, which the FDA approved for limited use in 2004.

Revolutionary Technology

While Herbert Boyer was turning bacteria into protein factories, Stanley Cohen improved techniques for using the microbes as photocopiers, producing multiple copies of genes for scientific study. Cohen has remained active at Stanford, where he is the Kwoh-Ting Li Professor of Genetics as well as a professor of medicine. Boyer, by contrast, retired from UCSF in 1991 and left scientific research behind. The two scientists shared many awards for their work, including the Albert Lasker Basic Medical Research Award (1980), the Helmut Horten Research Award from Switzerland (1993), and the Lemelson-MIT Prize for inventors (1996). Both were elected to the U.S. National Academy of Sciences and inducted into the National Inventors Hall of Fame in 2001. Cohen received the National Medal of Science in 1988 and Boyer in 1990, and both received the National Medal of Technology in 1989. In 2004, they were awarded the Albany Medical Center Prize, a grant of $500,000—the most monetarily valuable prize for medicine and biomedical research in the United States.

This long list of awards stresses how important the technology that Boyer and Cohen began creating in the Hawaiian delicatessen has become. Genetic engineering has produced life-saving medicines, new kinds of food, and—not least—a completely new way of studying genes and the way they work in the body. "Gene splicing is the most powerful and awesome skill acquired by man since the splitting of the atom," *Time* reporter Frederick Golden wrote in 1981. Much later, when awarding the two scientists the Lemelson-MIT Prize, Charles M. Vest, the president of the Massachusetts Institute of Technology (MIT), said, "Boyer and Cohen's ingenuity has revolutionized the way all of us live our lives."

Chronology

1935	Stanley Norman Cohen born in Perth Amboy, New Jersey, on February 17
1936	Herbert Wayne Boyer born in Derry, Pennsylvania, on July 10
1960	Cohen earns M.D. degree from University of Pennsylvania School of Medicine
1963	Boyer earns Ph.D. from University of Pittsburgh
1965	Scientists discover that bacteria contain small, ring-shaped pieces of DNA called plasmids in addition to their main genome
1966	Boyer joins faculty of University of California, San Francisco (UCSF)
1968	Cohen joins faculty of Stanford University
1971	Cohen devises way to make bacteria take up plasmids on demand
1972	Boyer and Cohen meet during a scientific conference in Hawaii in November and plan the first gene-splicing project
1973	Paul Berg combines genes from two kinds of viruses
	Robert Pollack warns Berg of possible danger from Berg's experiments, and Berg agrees to stop them

Boyer and Cohen combine pieces of genetic material from different types of bacteria, place the blended DNA into other bacteria, and show that the transplanted genes function

Berg and 77 other molecular biologists write letter to *Science*, urging that the National Academy of Sciences create safety standards for recombinant DNA research

1974	In July, *Science* publishes second letter from Berg and other scientists, in which they recommend a temporary halt to some gene-splicing experiments
1975	140 molecular biologists meet in Asilomar, California, from February 24 to February 27, to work out safety guidelines for genetic engineering
1976	National Institutes of Health draws up safety standards for recombinant DNA research and establishes Recombinant DNA Advisory Committee Herbert Boyer and Robert Swanson found Genentech, the first biotechnology company
1978	Genentech genetically engineers bacteria to make human insulin
1980	NIH drops most safety rules for recombinant DNA experiments Genentech stock is offered to the public and sells wildly Boyer and Cohen share Albert Lasker Award for Basic Medical Research
1982	Food and Drug Administration approves Genentech's recombinant human insulin for sale
1988	Stanley Cohen receives National Medal of Science
1989	Boyer and Cohen receive National Medal of Technology
1990	Herbert Boyer receives National Medal of Science
1991	Boyer retires from UCSF
2001	Boyer and Cohen elected to National Academy of Sciences and inducted into Inventors Hall of Fame
2004	Boyer and Cohen receive Albany Medical Center Prize

Further Reading

Books

Shorter, Edward. *The Health Century.* New York: Doubleday, 1987.
Chronicles the development of the National Institutes of Health
(NIH) and describes some of the important research that the institutes have sponsored. Includes description of NIH's role in the development of genetic engineering and early concerns about the safety of
this new technology.

Watson, James D., with Andrew Berry. *DNA: The Secret of Life.*
New York: Alfred A. Knopf, 2003.
History of research on DNA and genetics in the second half of the
20th century includes chapters on the birth of genetic engineering and
the development of the biotechnology industry.

Articles

Berg, Paul. "A Stanford Professor's Career in Biochemistry, Science
Politics, and the Biotechnology Industry." Available online. URL:
http://texts.cdlib.org/dynaxml/servlet/dynaXML?docId=kt1c600
1df&doc.view=entire_text. Accessed on November 12, 2004.
This series of interviews with Berg, conducted by Sally Smith Hughes
in 1997, is part of the UCSF Oral History Program and the Program
in the History of the Biological Sciences and Biotechnology, organized
by the Bancroft Library at the University of California, Berkeley. It
includes discussion of Berg's recombinant DNA research and the
Asilomar conference, which Berg helped organize.

———, et al. "Potential Biohazards of Recominant DNA Molecules,"
Science, 26 July 1974, p. 303.
Letter in which Berg, Boyer, Cohen, and others call for a temporary
halt to certain types of recombinant DNA experiments.

Boyer, Herbert. "Recombinant DNA Research at UCSF and
Commercial Applications by Genentech." Available online. URL:
http://texts.cdlib.org/dynaxml/servlet/dynaXML?docId=kt5d5nb0
zs&doc.view=entire_text. Accessed on November 11, 2004.
This series of interviews with Boyer, conducted by Sally Smith Hughes
in 1994, is part of the UCSF Oral History Program and the Program
in the History of the Biological Sciences and Biotechnology, organized

by the Bancroft Library at the University of California, Berkeley. It includes discussion of the invention of genetic engineering and the founding of Genentech.

Cohen, S. N., and others. "Construction of Biologically Functional Bacterial Plasmids in Vitro," *Proceedings of the National Academy of Sciences* 70 (November 1973): 3,240–3,344.

Scientific paper describing the construction of the first genetically engineered plasmids.

Golden, Frederick. "Shaping Life in the Lab," *Time,* 9 March 1981, pp. 50–56.

Conveys some of the excitement surrounding early commercial genetic engineering and biotechnology.

Miller, Julie Ann. "Lessons from Asilomar," *Science News* 127 (February 23, 1985): 122–124.

Written 10 years after the conference at Asilomar, California, during which molecular biologists drew up safety guidelines for genetic engineering experiments, this article recalls the meeting and discusses its effects.

Morrow, J. F., and others. "Replication and Transcription of Eukaryotic DNA in *Escherichia coli,*" *Proceedings of the National Academy of Sciences* 71 (May 1, 1974): 1,743–1,747.

Scientific paper demonstrating that recombinant DNA placed in a bacterium can function in its new location.

Web Sites

Access Excellence: About Biotech: Biotech Chronicles: Pioneer Profiles. Sponsored by the National Health Museum, this site for health and bioscience teachers and learners includes a history of biotechnology and biographical sketches of the industry's pioneers. Herbert Boyer is among those profiled. http://www.accessexcellence.org/RC/AB/BC/Herbert_Boyer.html. Accessed on November 11, 2004.

THE KILLERS INSIDE

MICHAEL BISHOP, HAROLD VARMUS, AND GENES THAT CAUSE CANCER

Famed British writer Robert Louis Stevenson's *The Strange Case of Dr. Jekyll and Mr. Hyde* is one of the most popular mysteries of all time. The book's main character, physician Henry Jekyll, is respected by all who know him—yet when Jekyll drinks a potion brewed in his laboratory, he is transformed into a brutal killer. In 1976, 90 years after Stevenson's book was published, two scientists in California discovered that transformations much like the one that turned Jekyll into the evil Mr. Hyde lie behind cancer, one of humankind's most feared diseases.

Accidental Scientists

Before they made their groundbreaking discovery, these two researchers, John Michael Bishop and Harold Eliot Varmus, went through some transformations of their own. Neither had planned to be a scientist when he was young. Bishop, born in the small town of York, Pennsylvania, on February 22, 1936, had thought about becoming a musician. (Even many years later, he wrote in the autobiographical sketch that he submitted to the Nobel Foundation that "if offered reincarnation, I would choose the career of a performing musician with exceptional talent, preferably, in a string quartet.") Feeling that he was not skilled enough for a career in music, however, Bishop majored in chemistry at Gettysburg College in Pennsylvania, from which he graduated in 1957. He became interested in research while attending Harvard Medical School. He earned his M.D. in 1962 and did postdoctoral work at the National Institutes of Health (NIH) and in Germany, specializing in viruses that cause cancer in animals.

Born on December 19, 1939, in Oceanside, a town on Long Island, New York, Harold Varmus grew up in nearby Freeport. He was attracted to both medicine and literature as a young man. Planning to follow in the footsteps of his father, a physician, Varmus took premedical courses at Amherst College in Massachusetts, but he changed his major to English and graduated with a degree in that subject in 1961. He earned a master's degree in 17th-century

Harold Varmus helped show that cancer-causing genes came originally from normal cells. (Albert and Mary Lasker Foundation)

English literature from Harvard University a year later. By then, however, Varmus had come to feel that his friends in medical school were "more engaged with the real world," as he told *New York Times* reporter Natalie Angier in 1993, so he decided to become a physician after all. He earned his M.D. from Columbia University's College of Physicians and Surgeons in New York in 1966. Varmus, a conscientious objector, became interested in biomedical research in 1968, when the Public Health Service assigned him to work at NIH as an alternative to military service during the Vietnam War.

Bishop joined the faculty of the University of California at San Francisco (UCSF) as an assistant professor of microbiology in 1968. Varmus came to San Francisco in 1969 and met Bishop "almost by accident," Varmus said to *Science* magazine writer Jean L. Marx in 1989. The two "hit it off right away," Varmus told Marx, just as James Watson and Francis Crick had done when they met at Cambridge in 1951. Bishop and Varmus decided to work together, and Varmus joined Bishop's laboratory at UCSF in 1970.

Viral Terrorists

In the late 1960s and early 1970s, Bishop's laboratory was one of many studying cancer-causing viruses. Although no virus had yet been shown to cause cancer in humans, researchers widely believed that such viruses would be found and that they would be similar to the ones that produced the disease in animals.

Francis Peyton Rous, a New York researcher, had identified the first cancer suspected to be caused by a virus in 1910. (At the time, no one had actually seen a virus, but indirect evidence led scientists to predict their existence.) The virus that produced this cancer, a muscle tumor (sarcoma) in chickens, was later isolated and named the Rous sarcoma virus. Other viruses were found to cause cancer in mice, rats, cats, monkeys, and other animals. These viruses could also transform normal cells grown in the laboratory into wildly multiplying forms that had many features of cancer cells.

Researchers in the early 1970s found a form of the Rous sarcoma virus that had lost its power to cause cancer. Comparing this virus with the normal one, they found that the cancer-causing form had one large gene at the end of its tiny genome that the harmless type lacked. Somehow, the scientists reasoned, that gene must produce cancer when the virus inserted it into a cell's genome. They called the gene src, for sarcoma. Other scientists identified different cancer-causing genes in other viruses. Robert Huebner and George Todaro of the National Cancer Institute, part of NIH, gave all these genes the name *oncogenes,* after a Greek word meaning "cancer." Huebner and Todaro proposed that when tumor viruses infected cells, the viruses slipped oncogenes into the cells' genomes much as a terrorist might smuggle in a bomb to blow up a building or a plane.

These genetic "bombs," however, might not go off for centuries. Huebner and Todaro suggested that normal cell genomes contained

CONNECTIONS: CANCER TO AIDS

Most viruses that cause cancer in animals belong to an unusual group called retroviruses ("backward viruses"). They were given this name because their genetic material is made of RNA rather than DNA. Instead of copying their DNA into RNA, as most living things do, retroviruses copy their RNA genomes into DNA and insert the DNA copy into the genomes of the cells they infect. When an infected cell copies its DNA before reproducing, it copies the virus's inserted genes as well. In this way, it makes more viruses.

In the 1960s and 1970s, many researchers were sure that sooner or later, someone would discover retroviruses that infect humans. Some thought that such viruses would prove to be a common cause of human cancer. Robert Gallo of the National Institutes of Health found the first human retrovirus in 1981 and showed that it caused a type of leukemia, a blood cancer. Gallo called the new virus HTLV, short for human T-cell leukemia virus. Shortly afterward he found a related virus that he named HTLV-2.

Only a few viruses have been proved to cause human cancers, and the types of cancer they trigger are uncommon. The discoveries that Gallo and others made about retroviruses became important in another way, however. Around the time Gallo discovered HTLV, medical journals were beginning to describe mysterious clusters of infections that attacked homosexual men. Researchers found that these men's immune systems had been destroyed. Scientists suspected that the cause of the disease was a retrovirus.

Gallo and his coworkers noticed that the mystery disease appeared to be transmitted in the same ways and affected the same cells as the leukemia produced by HTLV, and Gallo began to wonder whether a relative of HTLV might cause the new illness. His earlier work with the cancer retroviruses helped him isolate the virus that causes what came to be known as AIDS (acquired immuno-deficiency syndrome) in 1983. Luc Montagnier and others at the Pasteur Institute in France independently discovered the virus, later called HIV (human immunodeficiency virus), at the same time. As Gallo had suspected, HIV proved to be a retrovirus similar to HTLV, and earlier discoveries about cancer-causing retroviruses helped scientists both to learn how HIV attacks immune system cells and to develop treatments for AIDS.

potential oncogenes, which they called proviruses. The researchers theorized that these proviruses had been placed into the cells during viral infection in the distant evolutionary past and were passed on to descendants along with the cells' other genes. The proviruses caused cancer only if activated by exposure to agents that changed DNA, such as X-rays or certain chemicals.

Turning a Theory Upside Down

Bishop and Varmus decided to test Huebner and Todaro's theory. Dominique Stehelin, a French researcher working in their laboratory, made copies of the src gene from the Rous sarcoma virus. He then labeled the genes with a radioactive tracer and mixed them with single-stranded DNA from the cells of healthy chickens. If a form of src existed in the genome of the chicken cells, the labeled src would stick to it and mark its location.

In 1976, Stehelin and others in Bishop and Varmus's laboratory found a gene similar to src in normal chicken cells. To their amazement, further analysis showed that this src-like gene had the form of a cell gene, not a virus gene. They also found that the gene was active in the cells, even though the cells were not cancerous. In other words, src, or a gene almost identical to it, apparently was, or had been, a normal chicken gene. Before tumor viruses became terrorists, the researchers concluded, the viruses had been thieves, taking a potential killer gene from the cells themselves. Bishop and Varmus called the normal form of

J. Michael Bishop has said, "We carry the seeds of our cancer within us." (University of California, San Francisco)

src a cellular oncogene because the cell gene, like the viral form, could cause cancer under the right circumstances.

Turning Huebner and Todaro's theory on its head was only the first of the surprises that Bishop and Varmus's laboratory produced. Another researcher working with them, Deborah Spector, soon found versions of src in fish, birds, and mammals, including humans. The fact that the gene was so widespread meant that it had remained the same throughout a long period of evolution. That would happen only if the gene had an essential role in normal cells.

Activating Oncogenes

During the early 1980s, scientists in Bishop and Varmus's laboratory and elsewhere discovered that the cellular forms of src and other oncogenes played vital parts in the processes by which cells grow and divide. These genes are active only occasionally in most normal cells, but in cancer cells, the genes are "turned on" all the time. This constant activity pushes the cells into endless growth.

Cancer researchers learned that even a tiny mutation, or change in the sequence of bases in a gene, can transform the gene from a healthy Dr. Jekyll into a cancer-causing Mr. Hyde. In 1981, Robert Weinberg of the Whitehead Institute, part of the Massachusetts Institute of Technology (MIT), found an oncogene called ras in a human bladder tumor—the first oncogene isolated from a human cancer. When Weinberg and his coworkers analyzed the normal and cancer-causing forms of the ras gene, they found that the two differed by only one base. This minute difference, which the laboratory reported in 1983, apparently was enough to produce a major change in the protein that the gene made. Sunlight, X-rays, carcinogens (cancer-causing chemicals), and viruses can all cause mutations.

In other cases, scientists have found, a cellular oncogene becomes able to cause cancer when it moves from one chromosome, or one spot in a chromosome, to another. The move may place the oncogene next to another gene that signals the oncogene to become active, for instance. A cellular oncogene can also be turned on at the

OTHER SCIENTISTS: ROBERT WEINBERG (1942–)

Robert Allan Weinberg, born on November 11, 1942, grew up in Pittsburgh, Pennsylvania. He has spent essentially all of his career at the Massachusetts Institute of Technology (MIT), studying cancer. After Michael Bishop and Harold Varmus showed that oncogenes came originally from cells rather than viruses, Weinberg's laboratory began to look for such genes in human cancers. These cancers had been caused by carcinogenic chemicals, not viruses. Ironically, however, the oncogene that Weinberg's group found in one such tumor in 1981 proved to be identical to a gene found earlier in virus-caused tumors in rats. This cancer-causing gene had been named ras, for "rat sarcoma."

Weinberg's laboratory has remained in the forefront of research on cancer-causing genes for more than two decades. In 1983, the Weinberg team identified the tiny mutation that turned the oncogene ras from a normal cell growth gene into a killer. A researcher in Weinberg's group identified the first gene belonging to a second type of cancer-causing genes, the tumor suppressor genes, a few years later. Tumor suppressor genes slow or stop cell growth, and cancer can result when mutations keep the genes from functioning. In the 1990s, Weinberg's laboratory discovered still other genes that play a part in cancer, including one that helps keep cells from dying by rebuilding the ends of their chromosomes, which normally shorten over time.

Weinberg's work has earned many awards, including the Bristol-Meyers Award for Distinguished Achievement in Cancer Research (1984), Canada's Gairdner Foundation International Award (1992), and the National Medal of Science (1997). In 1999, Weinberg won the Killian Faculty Award from MIT, the highest honor the faculty can bestow on a member.

wrong time when stretches of DNA called promoters are inserted before and after it. A third way of activating cellular oncogenes is through gene amplification, in which extra copies of a gene are accidentally made. All these copies can make protein, so the result is a larger than normal amount of the gene's protein. Any of these moves and misplacements can occur when cells copy their DNA before reproducing.

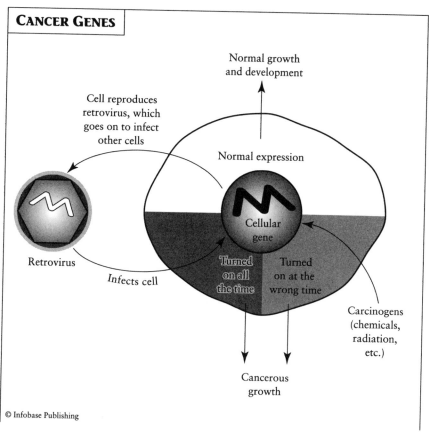

CANCER GENES

Normal growth and development

Cell reproduces retrovirus, which goes on to infect other cells

Normal expression

Retrovirus

Cellular gene

Infects cell

Turned on all the time

Turned on at the wrong time

Carcinogens (chemicals, radiation, etc.)

Cancerous growth

© Infobase Publishing

Michael Bishop and Harold Varmus found that cancer-causing genes, or onco-genes, were originally normal genes that played vital roles in cells' growth and development. Sometimes retroviruses accidentally captured these genes when the viruses infected cells. Long afterward, other retroviruses carrying the genes can trigger cancer when they infect new cells and insert the genes back into the cells' genomes. Alternatively, carcinogens can produce mutations that change a normal cell gene to an oncogene. Oncogenes differ from the normal form of the same genes in that the oncogenes either produce their proteins all the time or produce them at the wrong time in the cells' life cycle.

The Opposite of Oncogenes

As if oncogenes were not enough, scientists in the early 1980s discovered a second type of gene that can play a role in starting cancer. These genes are the exact opposite of oncogenes: Instead of producing cell growth, their normal job is preventing it. They cause cancer not when they become overactive, as happens with oncogenes, but when they fail to function. Cancer researchers call these genes tumor suppressor genes. Robert Weinberg has often said that active oncogenes are like a stuck accelerator on a car, whereas missing tumor suppressor genes are the equivalent of defective brakes.

Researchers found the first tumor suppressor gene in a rare type of cancer that strikes young children. This cancer, called retinoblastoma, grows in the eye. When an infant develops retinoblastoma, doctors usually have to remove one or both of the child's eyes in order to save its life.

Physicians had observed that retinoblastoma sometimes ran in families, but in other cases the cancer developed in children who had no relatives with the disease. Living things that reproduce sexually inherit two copies of each gene, one from the father and one from the mother. In 1971, Alfred G. Knudson, Jr., a professor of medical genetics and pediatrics at the Health Science Center in Houston, Texas, proposed that both copies of some gene, then unknown, were defective in retinoblastoma. Children from families in which the disease was common, he theorized, inherited one faulty copy of the gene and later lost the second copy through random mutation, perhaps when eye cells multiplied rapidly after birth. Children from families in which retinoblastoma had been unknown, on the other hand, inherited two normal genes, but mutations made both genes inactive. If both genes were inactivated in even one cell, that cell would begin multiplying uncontrollably and produce a tumor.

But what gene was missing? Jorge Yunis of the University of Minnesota Medical School found a clue in 1980 when he learned that a part of chromosome 13 was absent in all the cells of children with inherited retinoblastoma but only in the tumor cells of those with the noninherited form of the disease. Using techniques similar to those that had helped Bishop and Varmus find the normal form of the src gene, several sets of scientists

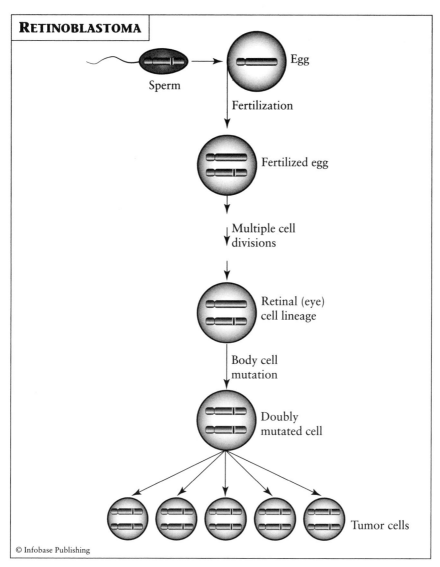

RETINOBLASTOMA

Sperm

Egg

Fertilization

Fertilized egg

Multiple cell divisions

Retinal (eye) cell lineage

Body cell mutation

Doubly mutated cell

Tumor cells

© Infobase Publishing

The damaged genes that result in the eye cancer called retinoblastoma are some-times inherited and sometimes not. In the example here, a child inherits one damaged gene (vertical bar) from its father. If a mutation damages the healthy gene (inherited from the mother) while eye cells are multiplying before birth, the cell in which the mutation occurs will lose the power to control its growth. It will multiply and form a tumor. A tumor can also result if both copies of the gene are normal when inherited from the parents but become damaged before birth.

began searching chromosome 13 for a gene that suppressed cell growth. Stephen H. Friend, a member of Robert Weinberg's laboratory, finally located the gene in 1986 and named it Rb, for retinoblastoma. The Rb gene has since been found in a variety of tissues, and it has proved to be missing in several different kinds of cancer.

After the discovery of Rb, scientists found a number of other tumor suppressor genes. One such gene, p53, is mutated or absent in a wide variety of cancers, including colon, bladder, and breast cancer. Unlike the case with Rb, even a single defective copy of p53 makes a cell produce a misshaped protein. As with proteins made by oncogenes, those made by tumor suppressor genes are part of complex chains of signals that control a cell's activities. A break or change in any link of one of these chains can keep the whole chain from working properly.

Many Steps to Cancer

Researchers have learned that more than one change in genes is almost always required to start a cancer. In the late 1980s, for instance, Bert Vogelstein of Johns Hopkins University in Baltimore, Maryland, found that at least four different mutations—activation of one oncogene and inactivation of three tumor suppressor genes, including p53—are required to produce a cancer in the colon (large intestine). If cancer were a gun, the first mutation would put a bullet in the chamber, the second take the safety catch off, the third cock the trigger, and the fourth fire the weapon. These changes may occur years apart and arise from different causes, which is why cancers usually take many years to develop and why most cancers occur in older people.

Sometimes potential cancer-causing mutations take place in the genes of the reproductive cells (eggs or sperm) and are passed on to offspring, giving the offspring an increased risk of cancer. In other cases, environmental factors such as carcinogens damage genes in particular body cells during an individual's lifespan. Cells can usually repair such damage, but if unrepaired changes occur in even a single cell, a tumor may start.

Most of the time, both heredity and environment play a role in starting cancer. A person might inherit one kind of mutated gene, for instance, but will not develop a tumor unless a second or even a third gene is damaged by environmental factors. Environment, however, is more important than heredity in causing most cancers.

From Research to Administration

Although Michael Bishop and Harold Varmus still worked together from time to time, Varmus had his own laboratory at UCSF after 1984. He remained at the university until 1993, doing research on oncogenes and on viruses such as the hepatitis B virus, which causes a serious liver disease.

Both men still lead research laboratories in the mid-2000s. Bishop's laboratory tries to learn what oncogenes and tumor suppressor genes do and how they do it in both normal and cancerous cells. Bishop says that his group's goal is to learn how normal cells control their growth and reproduction and why cancer cells fail to do so. Varmus's laboratory focuses on reproducing human cancers in genetically altered mice. It also uses gene alteration to study how cancer arises.

Varmus and Bishop themselves have little time for research, however, because both have gone on to highly respected careers in administration. Bishop became chancellor of UCSF in 1998. He also heads the G. W. Hooper Research Foundation, is a member of the Herbert Boyer Program in Biological Sciences, and is a university professor, the highest faculty level in the University of California. Varmus was the director of the National Institutes of Health from 1993 to 1999. Since 2000 he has been chief executive officer of the Memorial Sloan-Kettering Cancer Center in New York City, the oldest and largest private cancer research institution in the United States.

Varmus and Bishop have been showered with awards, many of them shared. Most important, they won the 1989 Nobel Prize in physiology or medicine. They also received the Albert Lasker Award for Basic Medical Research in 1982 and the Armand Hammer Cancer Research Prize, the Alfred P. Sloan, Jr., Prize from the

---

SOCIAL IMPACT: CANCER AND LIFESTYLE

Most researchers now believe that many cancers are the result of lifestyle choices, such as deciding to smoke cigarettes. A 1996 report from the Harvard School of Public Health claimed that 30 percent of human cancers result from tobacco use and another 30 percent from obesity (being severely overweight) and poor diet.

A strong statistical link between tobacco smoking and certain cancers, especially lung cancer, has been known since the 1950s, and several chemicals that could produce cancer in animals were found in tobacco smoke. Scientists did not know exactly how tobacco smoke caused cancer, however, until October 1996, when researchers from Texas and California showed that a carcinogen in tobacco smoke damages the p53 tumor suppressor gene in lung cells. This kind of damage has been found in many lung tumors.

Diet seems to affect the risk of developing colon cancer and perhaps other cancers. Diets high in fat, alcohol, and charred or pickled meats increase cancer risk. On the other hand, diets containing large quantities of fruits and vegetables reduce risk. Fruits and vegetables such as blueberries and broccoli contain compounds that keep carcinogens from damaging DNA.

Some critics, however, say that politicians and the media are too eager to "blame the victims" for cancer. These commentators believe that carcinogens from industrial pollution play as important a role in triggering cancer as carcinogens in food and cigarettes. For instance, organochlorines, which are found in pesticides, plastics, and many other commonly used materials, have been shown to disrupt the action of hormones in human and animal bodies. Unusually large numbers of women with breast cancer have been found in certain areas where organochlorine pollution is high, and some researchers theorize that exposure to such pollution raises the risk of developing breast cancer and perhaps other cancers.

General Motors Cancer Foundation, and the Gairdner Foundation International Award, all in 1984. Bishop was given the National Medal of Science in early 2005, and Varmus won two prestigious awards, the National Science Foundation's Vannevar Bush Award for lifetime achievement in science and public service and the National Medal of Science, in 2001.

A Complex Picture

In *Natural Obsessions,* her book on cancer research in the 1970s and 1980s, Natalie Angier quotes Tony Hunter of the Salk Institute in La Jolla, California, as saying, "As complicated as we think things are [in cancer research], they're sure to be more complicated than that." New discoveries have proved Hunter right. In 2004, for instance, researchers in California and France found a third type of cancer-related gene, called a conditional tumor suppressor. These genes sometimes slow tumor growth and sometimes speed it up, depending on their interaction with a certain protein in cells.

No matter how complex the picture of cancer causation becomes, however, the basic truth behind this frightening illness is the one that Michael Bishop and Harold Varmus first uncovered in 1976: Whether cancer is inherited or triggered by something in the environment, the disease always begins with changes in genes. In a *Science News* article published at the time Bishop and Varmus won the Nobel Prize, A. MacKenzie quoted fellow Nobel Prize winner David Baltimore as saying, "[Their] work gave us a new way of thinking about cancer. Until they made their discoveries, there was only speculation that cancer had a genetic component. Now there is a certainty." Ultimately, cancer comes not from an attack by an outside enemy but from a crazed revolt within the body itself. As Michael Bishop said to Natalie Angier, "We carry the seeds of our cancer within us."

Chronology

1910	Francis Peyton Rous theorizes that a type of chicken cancer is caused by a virus
1936	John Michael Bishop born in York, Pennsylvania, on February 22

1939	Harold Eliot Varmus born in Oceanside, New York, on December 19
1962	Bishop earns M.D. from Harvard Medical School Varmus earns master's degree in 17th-century English literature from Harvard University
1966	Varmus earns M.D. from Columbia University College of Physicians and Surgeons
1968	Bishop joins faculty of University of California at San Francisco (UCSF)
1969	Bishop and Varmus meet
1970	Varmus joins Bishop's laboratory
1970s	Early in the decade, Robert Huebner and George Todaro theorize that cancer arises when oncogenes that viruses inserted into cells in the distant past are activated
1970s	Late in the decade, Deborah Spector finds normal forms of oncogenes in a wide variety of living things, suggesting that these genes do important work in cells
1971	Alfred G. Knudson, Jr., theorizes that retinoblastoma, an eye tumor, is caused by inactivation of both copies of an unknown gene
1976	Bishop and Varmus's laboratory finds a normal cell gene that resembles an oncogene and theorizes that oncogenes originate in normal cells
1980s	Early in the decade, researchers learn different jobs that the normal form of oncogenes do in cells and different mechanisms by which oncogenes may be changed to a cancer-causing form
1981	Robert Weinberg finds an oncogene in a human cancer
1982	Bishop and Varmus win Albert Lasker Award for Basic Medical Research
1983	Robert Weinberg's laboratory reports that normal and cancer-causing forms of the ras oncogene differ by only one base

1984	Harold Varmus given his own laboratory at UCSF
	Varmus and Bishop receive several major awards
1986	Stephen H. Friend, a researcher in Robert Weinberg's laboratory, identifies Rb (for retinoblastoma), the first known tumor suppressor gene
late 1980s	Researchers discover additional tumor suppressor genes
	Bert Vogelstein shows that at least four different mutations are required to cause colon cancer
1989	Bishop and Varmus win Nobel Prize in physiology or medicine
1993	Varmus becomes director of National Institutes of Health
1998	Bishop becomes chancellor of UCSF
1999	Varmus resigns directorship of National Institutes of Health
2000	Varmus becomes chief executive officer of Memorial Sloan-Kettering Cancer Center
2001	Varmus wins National Medal of Science and National Science Foundation's Vannevar Bush Award
2004	Conditional tumor suppressor genes, a third class of cancer-related gene, discovered
2005	Bishop awarded National Medal of Science

Further Reading

Books

Angier, Natalie. *Natural Obsessions*. New York: Warner Books, 1988.
Book on breakthroughs in cancer research in the 1970s and 1980s focuses on Robert Weinberg's laboratory but also includes information on discoveries made by Bishop and Varmus.
Bishop, J. Michael. *How to Win a Nobel Prize: An Unexpected Life in Science*. Cambridge, Mass.: Harvard University Press, 2003.

Includes autobiographical material, a summary of scientific discoveries about infectious diseases and cancer, and thoughts about the relationship of scientists to politicians and the public.

Varmus, Harold, and Robert A. Weinberg. *Genes and the Biology of Cancer.* New York: Scientific American Library, 1993.
Well-illustrated book describes discoveries in the cellular biology of cancer. Somewhat difficult reading.

Articles

Angier, Natalie. "Harold E. Varmus: Out of the Lab and into the Bureaucracy," *New York Times,* 23 November 1993, pp. B5, C1.
Profile and interview with Varmus at the time he became director of the National Institutes of Health.

Bishop, J. Michael. "J. Michael Bishop—Autobiography." *Les Prix Nobel 1989.* Available online. URL: http://nobelprize.org/medicine/laureates/1989/bishop-autobio.html. Accessed on December 2, 2004.
Autobiographical sketch written when Bishop won a share of the 1989 Nobel Prize in physiology or medicine.

———. "Oncogenes," *Scientific American,* March 1982, pp. 80–92.
Describes the nature and discovery of oncogenes. Somewhat difficult reading.

Fallows, James. "The Political Scientist," *New Yorker,* 7 June 1999, pp. 66–74.
Lengthy review of Harold Varmus's tenure as director of the National Institutes of Health.

McKenzie, A. "Gene-Tracking Leads to Nobel Prize," *Science News,* 7 October 1989, p. 244.
Reports on the 1989 winners of the Nobel Prize in physiology or medicine.

Marx, Jean L. "Cancer Gene Research Wins Medicine Nobel," *Science,* 20 October 1989, pp. 326–327.
Describes the research that won Bishop and Varmus a Nobel Prize.

Stehelin, Dominique, et al. "DNA Related to the Transforming Gene(s) of Avian Sarcoma Viruses Is Present in Normal Avian DNA," *Nature,* 11 March 1976, pp. 170–173.
Scientific paper reporting discovery that the oncogene src appeared to have originated in normal chicken cells.

Varmus, Harold E. "Harold E. Varmus—Autobiography," *Les Prix Nobel 1989*. Available online. URL: http://nobelprize.org/medicine/laureates/1989/varmus-autobio.html. Accessed on December 2, 2004.
Autobiographical sketch written when Varmus won a share of the 1989 Nobel Prize in physiology or medicine.
"Varmus, Harold E." *Current Biography Yearbook 1996*. New York: H. W. Wilson, 1996.
Biographical profile of Varmus, with many quotes from interviews, covers both his scientific work and his term as director of the National Institutes of Health.

NEW GENES FOR OLD

FRENCH ANDERSON AND GENE THERAPY

In 1958, just five years after James Watson and Francis Crick had described the structure of DNA, a Harvard graduate student went to a seminar. He listened to a visiting professor describe new discoveries about the structure of hemoglobin, the red protein in the blood that carries oxygen. In *Correcting the Code,* a book describing the birth of gene therapy, Larry Thompson reports that the young man said,

> *If it is possible to work out the structure of normal hemoglobin, then maybe you can work out the structure of sickle cell hemoglobin [the defective hemoglobin in the bodies of people with sickle-cell anemia, a common inherited disease], and then you could determine what the defect is. And . . . maybe you could put in the gene for normal hemoglobin, and correct sickle cell hemoglobin.*

The professor was not interested in such a novel idea. "This is a serious scientific discussion," he snapped. "If you want to daydream, keep it to yourself!"

The rejection hurt, of course. It did not stop the student, W. French Anderson, from daydreaming about curing human disease by replacing damaged genes, however, nor did it persuade him to keep his idea to himself. Instead, he pursued his dream of gene therapy relentlessly until, in 1990, he began to make it come true. In that year, for the first time, a child with an inherited disease was started on the road to health by a change made in her genes.

Boyhood Dreams

William French Anderson, born in Tulsa, Oklahoma, on December 31, 1936, outpaced most of his classmates in school. While other students struggled with grade-school readers, he devoured college textbooks. By Anderson's own admission, quoted in his *Current Biography Yearbook 1994* profile, he was "a rather weird little boy." When he was in fifth grade, a classmate told him that he was the most unpopular boy in the school.

Anderson decided to change that. First, to mark his new personality, he changed the name he used from Bill to his middle name, French. He then set about making friends with the same energy and determination that he would later use to blaze the trail for a new medical treatment. By seventh grade he was well liked enough to be elected class president.

French Anderson had planned to be a physician since he was 10 years old. By the time he finished high school, he knew that he wanted to do research rather than treat patients. He learned about Watson and Crick's discovery of DNA's structure just before he applied to Harvard University in 1953, and at that time, he told Jeff Lyon and Peter Gorner when they interviewed him for their book on gene therapy, *Altered Fates,* he made himself two promises: "I was going to be in the Olympics, and I was going to cure defective molecules."

W. *French Anderson led the team that performed the first approved, successful gene therapy on a human.* (French Anderson)

From the start of his career, Anderson worked with top scientists. He met James Watson at Harvard, from which he graduated in 1958, and he did graduate work under Francis Crick at Cambridge. Anderson earned his master's degree from Cambridge in 1960 and returned to Harvard for his medical degree in 1963. In 1965, he moved to the National Institutes of Health (NIH) and joined the laboratory of Marshall Nirenberg, the leader among the researchers deciphering the genetic code. Larry Thompson reports that Anderson's enthusiasm and reliability soon made Nirenberg call Anderson his "right-hand man."

Anderson first helped people who had an inherited disease in 1968. The illness was thalassemia, a rare blood disorder that, like the more common sickle-cell disease, was caused by a defect in one of the genes that make hemoglobin. Anderson developed a treatment that helped people with thalassemia live longer, but it did not cure the disease or repair the faulty gene that lay at the illness's root. Anderson stopped this line of research in 1974 because it was not bringing him closer to his goal of gene therapy.

A Devastating Disease

When genetic engineering was invented in the early 1970s, Anderson hoped that his dream of repairing human genes was moving closer to reality. He and many other researchers found, however, that the gene transfer techniques that succeeded so well in bacteria did not work with human cells. Only in 1984 did a Massachusetts Institute of Technology (MIT) scientist, Richard Mulligan, invent a way to use retroviruses to introduce genes into the cells of mammals. Retroviruses are natural genetic engineers, reproducing by inserting their genomes into cells and making the cells copy the viruses' genetic material along with their own, but they can cause cancer and other dangerous diseases. To make the viruses safe, Mulligan removed the genes that allowed the viruses to reproduce and cause disease. He then substituted the genes that he wanted to transfer. The viruses inserted the new genes into the cells with the rest of their genomes.

Anderson immediately began planning ways to adapt Mulligan's technique to the treatment of genetic diseases. First, he had to decide

CONNECTIONS: GOOD NEWS–BAD NEWS GENES

Scientists have wondered why the genes that cause inherited diseases such as thalassemia and sickle-cell anemia have survived so long in certain groups of people, since the diseases normally kill their victims at an early age. An interesting theory to explain this puzzle has emerged.

Most inherited diseases are caused by recessive genes, which means that a child will become ill only if he or she inherits defective copies of the disease-causing gene from both parents. People who inherit one defective and one normal copy of the gene will be quite healthy. Such people are called carriers because they can potentially carry or transmit the disease to their children, even though they are not sick themselves.

Under some circumstances, the theory goes, carriers of the genes for thalassemia or certain other blood diseases may actually be healthier than people who inherit two normal genes. Research has shown that people who inherit one defective copy of the gene for thalassemia or sickle-cell anemia seem to be more resistant to malaria, a serious blood infection caused by a microorganism, than people who have only normal genes. These inherited blood disorders usually occur in people whose ancestors came from the Mediterranean Sea area or Africa, where malaria is common. The damaged genes may thus have given their carriers an evolutionary advantage, even though some of their children died.

which disease to work with. He knew that the sickness he chose must be caused by a defect in just one gene, because inserting even a single gene into cells and making the gene function there would be tricky. The identity of the gene had to be known so that it could be mass-produced in the laboratory. Finally, the disease had to be treatable by inserting a gene into a relatively small number of cells that could easily be taken from and returned to the body, such as blood cells.

Only a few inherited illnesses met all these requirements. Anderson focused on one called ADA deficiency. This disease is very rare, affecting only about 40 people in the world at any given time, but it is deadly. The cells of people with ADA deficiency cannot make a chemical called adenosine deaminase (ADA), which certain blood cells in the immune system (the body's defense system) must have in order to survive. Without ADA, the immune system cannot function. Like people with AIDS, children with ADA deficiency suffered from infections almost constantly. Most died before they were two years old.

Moving toward Treatment

Knowing Anderson's interest in ADA deficiency, his wife, Kathy, a surgeon who specialized in treating children, introduced him to another NIH scientist, Michael Blaese. Blaese was an expert in ADA deficiency and other childhood immune diseases. He and Anderson began working together in 1984.

Anderson and Blaese hoped to treat ADA deficiency by placing the gene for making ADA into stem cells, long-lived cells in bone marrow that make all the cells in the blood, but they were unable to put the gene into these cells. In mid-1987, however, Don Kohn, a member of the Anderson-Blaese research team, successfully transferred the gene to white cells, immune system cells in the blood. White cells do not live as long as stem cells, but some kinds survive for a decade or more. The researchers decided that if they could get the ADA gene into enough of these cells, their treatment might be almost as good as one involving stem cells.

While other team members were struggling with the technical difficulties of the ADA project, Anderson took on the political ones. Before his group could try their novel treatment on a human being, he would have to win approval from both the federal Food and Drug Administration (FDA), which oversees all human tests of new medical treatments, and the Recombinant DNA Advisory Committee (RAC), which evaluates the safety of genetic engineering experiments. To gain the permissions he needed, Anderson would have to convince both agencies that his treatment would be effective and safe. The first time he applied to the RAC, in 1987, the committee rejected him, saying that the treatment needed more tests in animals.

Shortly afterward, another obstacle to Anderson's plans appeared in the form of a new treatment for ADA deficiency that seemed far less risky than gene therapy. ADA breaks down quickly in the body, so it cannot not be given by itself as a pill or a shot, but a researcher at Duke University in North Carolina found a way to combine it with a substance called polyethylene glycol. The resulting drug, PEG-ADA, could survive in the bloodstream, and weekly injections of PEG-ADA let some ADA-deficient children begin to lead relatively normal lives. Anderson learned, however, that the drug did not help all children with the disease. He still hoped he could persuade the RAC to let him try gene therapy with children who did not respond to PEG-ADA.

Small Step, Giant Leap

In 1988, Anderson and Blaese found a possible shortcut to approval for gene therapy that did not involve treatment of disease at all. It grew out of the work of another NIH scientist, Steven A. Rosenberg, chief of surgery at the National Cancer Institute. Rosenberg had found a type of immune system cell that attacked cancers, and he was trying to strengthen these cells by removing them from patients' blood, treating them with various substances, and reinjecting them. A few of his experiments had succeeded, but most had not, and he wanted to know why. To find out, he needed some way to mark the cells so their activities could be traced after they reentered his patients' bodies.

Blaese suggested to Rosenberg that adding a gene to the cells while they were in the laboratory might do the trick. Blaese recommended a gene that made cells resistant to neomycin, an antibiotic. Cells carrying this gene could be identified because they would grow in dishes containing neomycin, which most cells could not. Blaese and Anderson offered to work with Rosenberg to create the altered cells.

The resistance gene was not expected to have any effect on the patients or their cancers; its only purpose was to be a marker. This fact, along with Rosenberg's insistence that he would give gene-altered cells only to people already expected to die of cancer within

TRACKING CELLS WITH MARKERS

1. Immune system cells taken from cancer patients' blood

2. Cells strengthened in laboratory; neomycin resistance marker gene (●) added to cells

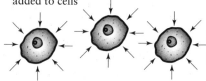

3. Cells reinjected into patients

4. Pieces of patients' tumors removed

5. Cells from tumors placed in dishes containing nutrients and neomycin

6. All cells die: No marked cells survived in this tumor   OR   Some cells survive: This tumor contained some cells bearing resistance gene

© Infobase Publishing

In the first genetically altered cells injected into humans, the added genes were simply markers. As part of an experimental treatment for cancer, Steven Rosenberg was attempting to strengthen immune system cells that attacked tumors. At French Anderson's suggestion, Rosenberg removed immune system cells from cancer patients' blood (1). Rosenberg added a gene conveying resistance to the antibiotic neomycin to these cells when he treated the cells in his laboratory (2). He then reinjected the cells into the patients from whom they had come (3). After a few days, Rosenberg removed pieces of the patients' tumors and put them in dishes containing neomycin (4). If any of his marked cells had reached the tumors, those cells would survive while the other cells, which lacked the resistance gene, would die (5). Rosenberg could thus learn whether his strengthened cells were migrating into the patients' tumors.

a few months, persuaded the RAC and the FDA to let him try the experiment. On May 22, 1989, the Rosenberg-Anderson team gave the first dose of altered cells to a truck driver with advanced melanoma, a deadly skin cancer. Jeff Lyon and Peter Gorner's book says that just after the treatment began, someone put up a sign in Anderson's lab that, echoing astronaut Neil Armstrong's first words after walking onto the Moon, read, "One small step for a gene, but a giant leap for genetics."

A Girl Called Ashanthi

The engineered cells did not seem to harm Rosenberg's patients, so Anderson's group began to hope that they might soon obtain the permission they needed for their more ambitious proposal. Blaese knew most of the ADA-deficient children in the United States, and from among these he chose the one who seemed most likely to benefit from the therapy. She was a solemn, round-faced three-year-old named Ashanthi DeSilva—Ashi for short. She and her parents, Raj and Van DeSilva, lived in Cleveland, Ohio, where Raj was a chemical engineer. Ashi's parents kept her at home, away from other children, in the hope of preventing the constant infections she had suffered almost since birth. She received regular PEG-ADA shots, but although the drug had helped her at first, it had seemingly lost its effectiveness.

Blaese and the other scientists began talking to the DeSilvas in May 1990. After considering the possible benefits and risks, which could include cancer if the viruses inserted their genetic cargo in the wrong place, Ashi's parents agreed to let her take the treatment. The RAC also granted its permission in summer 1990, and the FDA did the same in early September.

Historic Treatment

Ashanthi DeSilva and her parents came to NIH at the beginning of September 1990. French Anderson's research team removed blood from Ashi's arm on September 5, filtered out the white cells, and

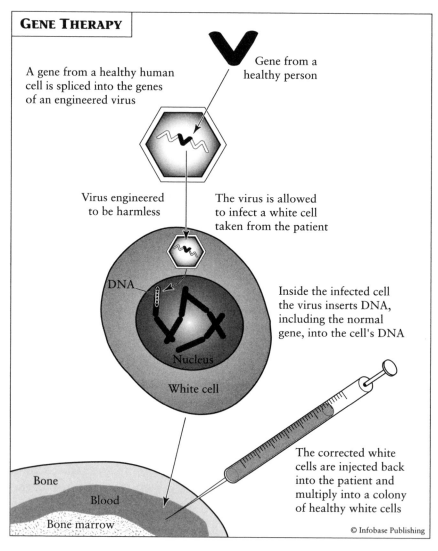

GENE THERAPY

A gene from a healthy human cell is spliced into the genes of an engineered virus

Gene from a healthy person

Virus engineered to be harmless

The virus is allowed to infect a white cell taken from the patient

DNA

Inside the infected cell the virus inserts DNA, including the normal gene, into the cell's DNA

Nucleus

White cell

Bone

Blood

Bone marrow

The corrected white cells are injected back into the patient and multiply into a colony of healthy white cells

© Infobase Publishing

To treat Ashanthi DeSilva, French Anderson and his coworkers used genetic engineering techniques to splice a human gene that makes ADA (dark segment) into the genome of a retrovirus. The virus had been modified so that it could not reproduce or cause disease. White cells were then removed from Ashanthi's blood and grown in laboratory dishes. The virus was added to the dishes and infected some of the cells, inserting the ADA gene into them along with the virus's own RNA. When the cells were injected back into Ashanthi, the new gene began making ADA in her body, allowing her immune system to function.

returned the red cells and fluid to her body. They then took the white cells to their laboratory, mixed them with viruses containing the ADA gene, and let the cells multiply for 10 days.

Finally, on September 14, just a few days past her fourth birthday, Ashi made medical history as she watched *Sesame Street* on the television near her hospital bed. Over the span of about half an hour, a billion or so of her own white blood cells dripped through a tube and needle into a vein in her hand. The procedure was much like an ordinary blood transfusion. Anderson and the other scientists at Ashi's bedside hoped, however, that this transfusion was bringing Ashi the lifesaving ADA gene.

Ashi's gene treatment had to be repeated every month at first. She also continued to receive PEG-ADA shots as a backup, in case the gene therapy failed. The dose, however, was eventually reduced to a quarter of its original amount. In August 1992, after 11 treatments, Anderson's group stopped the gene therapy because it no longer seemed necessary. The ADA gene apparently had entered some of Ashi's long-lived white cells, and the offspring of these cells were replacing enough of her defective ones to keep her healthy.

Laboratory tests confirmed that Ashi's immune system improved steadily in the months after her therapy began and was totally normal within a year. The girl gained energy and suffered fewer infections. Although not cured of her disease, she started attending school, playing with friends, and generally leading the life of a normal child. By 1995, Anderson wrote in a

French Anderson and Ashanthi DeSilva walk down a hospital corridor together after her historic treatment in September 1990. (French Anderson)

SOCIAL IMPACT: DESIGNER BABIES AND SUPERHUMANS

Joseph Levine and David Suzuki write in their book on modern genetic discoveries, *The Secret of Life,* that on the day of Ashanthi DeSilva's first gene treatment, French Anderson told reporters that the moment represented "a cultural breakthrough, . . . an event that changes the way that we as a society think about ourselves." From then on, he said, people would see their genes as something that potentially could be changed at will, not as a legacy that had to be accepted.

Not everyone likes that idea. Few people object to gene changes that would cure or prevent a potentially fatal illness like Ashanthi's, but critics such as Jeremy Rifkin have speculated that if modifying human genes ever becomes easy, gene alteration will not stop with treating disease. Would-be athletes might take gene treatments to build up their muscles or change their bodies in other ways that might give them an advantage in sports. Parents might demand that genes of their unborn children be altered or selected to prevent even minor defects, such as nearsightedness, or to enhance desirable qualities like intelligence. Gene enhancement—changing genes of basically healthy people in an attempt to make them "better"—could decrease human diversity or even result in a kind of genocide, if masses of parents chose to change their children's skin color, for instance. Because of these potential problems, French Anderson, for one, has said that gene treatments should be used only for preventing or curing serious illness.

Ethical questions will grow even greater if the genes in a person's sex cells (sperm and eggs), which are the only genes that can be passed on to children, are ever altered. So far, no gene treatment has intentionally done this. If Ashanthi DeSilva has children, for instance, they will not inherit the healthy ADA genes she has been given. Many ethicists and scientists think that germ-line, or inheritable, genes should never be changed, even to prevent disease. A change that seems desirable when it is made might have disastrous consequences for entire families many generations later.

Nonetheless, gene enhancement and alteration of germ-line genes have their supporters. Those who accept gene enhancement see it as no worse than, say, straightening a child's crooked teeth or sending the child to a private school. Some, including genetics pioneer James Watson, go even further, saying that changing germ-line genes could benefit the human race.

Scientific American article, Ashi had been "transformed from a quarantined little girl, who was always sick and left the house only to visit her doctor, into a healthy, vibrant nine-year-old who loves life and does *everything.*" In 2004, Ashanthi, then a young woman, was still healthy, and a quarter of her white cells carried normal ADA genes. Gene treatment of a second ADA-deficient child, Cynthia Cutshall, produced almost equally encouraging results.

Gene Therapy's Rocky Road

In the years following Ashi DeSilva's landmark treatment, French Anderson and other researchers experimented with changing or replacing genes to treat disease. They explored gene therapy, not only for inherited diseases like ADA deficiency, but for common illnesses that are not usually inherited but in which genes play a role, such as heart disease, cancer, and AIDS.

Unfortunately, DeSilva has remained one of gene therapy's few long-running success stories. Some treatments produced promising results in early tests but encountered problems later. For instance, some patients' immune systems destroyed the gene-carrying viruses before the genetic "delivery trucks" could do their work. In other cases, the patients became allergic to the viruses.

Enthusiasm for gene therapy reached a low point around the start of the 21st century because of two disastrous events. First, on September 17, 1999, a young man named Jesse Gelsinger died after receiving experimental gene therapy for an inherited liver disease. His death was probably caused by an immune reaction to a high dose of gene-carrying viruses. Then two children in France who had been given gene therapy for an immune system disease similar to DeSilva's developed leukemia in 2002. The therapy seemed to have cured the children's illness, but researchers concluded that viruses had inserted replacement genes in a spot that activated an oncogene, triggering the cancer.

These tragedies shook gene therapy to its roots. The RAC and other government agencies criticized a number of researchers for not reporting other cases in which gene treatments had produced harmful side effects. They greatly increased the strictness of the regulations governing the field. For a short time after leukemia was discovered in the children in France, the FDA shut down about a third of the human tests of gene therapy in the United States. Most

Issues: How Much Risk Is Acceptable?

Any new medical treatment is risky. To identify possible dangers, researchers test drugs or other new treatments on animals such as mice before giving them to human beings. The first human tests are usually done on small numbers of volunteer patients for whom no other treatment has been effective. These tests are not aimed at curing disease, but rather are designed to find out what side effects (harmful or unwanted effects) the treatment might have. If few side effects occur, the treatment will be given to larger numbers of patients. Any treatment must pass three stages of human tests before the FDA will allow it to be sold.

Before letting someone join a trial of a new treatment, researchers must give the person (or the person's parents, if he or she is a child) a form to sign. The form describes the treatment, any possible side effects that are known, and how likely those side effects are to occur. By signing the form, the person gives "informed consent," accepting the risks of the treatment. One criticism of some gene therapy trials, including the one involving Gelsinger, was that the consent forms used in them left out reports of some bad reactions that had occurred in previous tests. New regulations after Gelsinger's death strengthened the requirements for clear, complete consent forms.

Some gene therapy researchers fear that regulators will go too far in trying to eliminate risk. These scientists say that some harmful results, and even deaths, are unavoidable during the early stages of a treatment as revolutionary as gene therapy. "One [death] in 5,000 [the number of people given gene therapy treatments up to that time]—that is not a safety record to be disparaged," Michael Blaese told a *Business Week* reporter soon after Gelsinger's death. "Thousands of patients die from reactions to aspirin every year," Blaese asserted, yet no one suggests banning this common medication. Patients and their families have often said that they are willing to accept the risks of experimental treatments because their conditions are otherwise untreatable.

of the trials were later allowed to continue, but under much more careful supervision. In 2004, more than 900 trials of gene therapies on human beings were under way around the world.

In response to the many complaints leveled at gene therapy, researchers in the field have been working hard to restore its reputation and improve the safety of proposed treatments. Some are developing ways to introduce genes without using viruses, for example. "The field is basically on track," Katherine High, president of the American Society of Gene Therapy, insisted to *Scientist* writer Josh P. Roberts in September 2004.

Always an Optimist

Throughout gene therapy's roller-coaster ride between enthusiasm and disgrace, French Anderson has kept his belief that gene treatments will prove to be the best way to cure or prevent many illnesses. "It is his mission. He will not quit. He never entertains the possibility of failure," Anderson's wife, Kathy, told writers Bob Burke and Barry Epperson when they were preparing their biography of Anderson, *W. French Anderson: Father of Gene Therapy.*

Anderson himself continues to work toward gene therapy's acceptance. In 1992, he left the National Institutes of Health and moved to the University of Southern California, in Los Angeles, where today he heads the gene therapy laboratories at the university's Keck School of Medicine. He is also a professor of biochemistry and pediatrics at the medical school and a founder of a Maryland biotechnology company called Genetic Therapy, Inc.

Anderson's laboratory, like many others, is trying to make gene therapy both safer and more effective. His team is developing ways to use viruses that he hopes will overcome some of the problems encountered in the past, for instance. They are also working on techniques for introducing genes into stem cells. More controversially, Anderson has proposed treating babies for certain genetic diseases while they are still in their mother's wombs. Such treatment, he says, is the only way to keep these conditions from causing irreversible damage before birth. Some scientists and other critics oppose this treatment because it might alter genes in the unborn baby's sex cells, which could be passed on to future generations.

Although some people find his work disturbing, French Anderson has received many honors, including a Distinguished Service Award from the U.S. Department of Health and Human Services (1992), the King Faisal International Prize in Medicine (1994), the National Biotechnology Award (1995), and the Coudert Institute Award for Medical Sciences (2003). *Time* magazine named him one of its "Heroes of Medicine" in 1997. He was inducted into the Oklahoma Hall of Fame in 1998, and he has received five honorary doctorates.

Events like the death of Jesse Gelsinger and the illness of the children in France suggest that gene therapy may not become a common medical treatment for a long time. If it ever does succeed, however, it will surely do so in large part because of the persistence and determination of the onetime "daydreamer," French Anderson.

Chronology

1936	William French Anderson born in Tulsa, Oklahoma, on December 31
1963	Anderson earns medical degree from Harvard University
1965	Anderson joins Marshall Nirenberg's laboratory at National Institutes of Health and helps to decipher the genetic code
1968	Anderson begins work on thalassemia
1974	Anderson ends work on thalassemia because it is not leading to gene therapy
1984	Richard Mulligan invents a way to make retroviruses safe to use as vectors for carrying genes
	Anderson and Michael Blaese begin plans to treat ADA deficiency with gene therapy
1987	Don Kohn invents a way to put the ADA gene into white cells
	RAC rejects Anderson group's first proposal to perform gene therapy
	PEG-ADA, a drug to treat ADA deficiency, is created

1988	Anderson, Blaese, and Steven Rosenberg plan to use an added gene as marker in an experimental cancer treatment
1989	On May 22, Rosenberg group inserts foreign genes into human beings for the first time
1990	In the summer, RAC grants approval for Anderson's group to use gene therapy on a single ADA-deficient child
	The parents of the child, Ashanthi DeSilva, consent to the treatment
	On September 14, Anderson places genetically altered cells into DeSilva, providing the first approved use of gene therapy to treat disease
1992	French Anderson moves from National Institutes of Health to University of Southern California (Los Angeles)
	Ashanthi DeSilva's gene treatments end in August
1999	Jesse Gelsinger dies on September 17 as a result of experimental gene therapy
2002	Two children in France, seemingly cured of an immune system disorder by gene therapy, develop leukemia

Further Reading

Books

Burke, Bob, and Barry Epperson. *W. French Anderson: Father of Gene Therapy.* Oklahoma City, Okla.: Oklahoma Heritage Association, 2003.
   Biography of the scientist who pioneered gene therapy and remains one of its strongest supporters.
Levine, Joseph, and David Suzuki. *The Secret of Life.* Boston: WGBH Educational Foundation, 1993.
   Describes recent advances in genetics and genetic engineering.
Lyon, Jeff, and Peter Gorner. *Altered Fates.* New York: W. W. Norton, 1995.
   Describes the development of gene therapy, including experiments in the early 1990s after Ashanthi DeSilva's treatment.

Thompson, Larry. *Correcting the Code.* New York: Simon and Schuster, 1994.
 Focuses on French Anderson's work but also describes the advances in molecular biology and genetic engineering that made gene therapy possible.
Yount, Lisa. *Gene Therapy.* San Diego, Calif.: Lucent Books, 2002.
 For young adults. Recounts the development of gene therapy, experimental gene treatments for a variety of diseases, and controversies that rocked the field in the late 1990s.

Articles

Anderson, W. French. "Gene Therapy," *Scientific American,* September 1995, pp. 124–128.
 Fairly technical article describes Anderson's pioneering treatment of Ashanthi DeSilva.
"Anderson, W. French," *Current Biography Yearbook 1994,* 16–20. New York: H. W. Wilson, 1994.
 Good biographical article on Anderson, including quotes from several interviews.
"One Death in 5,000 Shouldn't Doom Gene Therapy," *Business Week,* 13 December 1999, p. 148.
 Editorial defending gene therapy against complaints following Jesse Gelsinger's death.
Roberts, Josh P. "Gene Therapy's Fall and Rise (Again)," *The Scientist,* 27 September 2004, pp. 22–24.
 Reviews the effect of tragedies involving gene therapy in 1999 and 2002 and the field's slow recovery. Somewhat technical.

5
DEATH IN THE FAMILY
NANCY WEXLER AND GENES FOR INHERITED DISEASES

Nancy Sabin Wexler, born July 19, 1945, in Washington, D.C., was just 23 years old on the fateful day in August 1968 when Milton Wexler, her father, asked her and her older sister, Alice, to come home for a serious talk. Milton Wexler had terrible news for his daughters: Leonore, their mother, had just been found to have an incurable brain ailment called Huntington's disease. The disease was inherited, he explained. Leonore's three brothers and her father, whose sickness and early deaths had always been mysteries to the young women, had died of it. After 10 or 15 years of slow mental degeneration, Leonore would die too. Perhaps worst of all, the laws of inheritance said that Nancy and Alice each had a 50-50 chance of developing the same illness.

Most people would have been devastated by such an announcement. After her first shock and grief wore off, however, Nancy Wexler vowed to fight the disease that threatened her and her family. "She went from being dismal to . . . wanting to be a knight in shining armor going out to fight the devils," Milton Wexler, a psychoanalyst, told Lauren Picker in an interview published in the March 1994 issue of *American Health*.

A Deadly Legacy

Milton and Leonore Wexler had divorced in 1964, but Leonore still talked to Milton about her problems because she considered

73

him a friend. She had told him about the police officer who accused her of being drunk because she staggered when she crossed a street. She had told him when a doctor finally found out what her real problem was.

Huntington's disease was named after George Huntington, the doctor who first described it in 1872, Milton Wexler explained to his daughters. It affects about 40,000 people in the United States. The illness causes shaking movements that turn into a grotesque, writhing "dance," memory loss, bursts of anger or violence, depression, and finally mental confusion. All these effects come from a single defective gene that destroys a small but vital area of the brain.

There is no cure or treatment for this relentless disease. One of its most tragic features is that signs of it usually do not appear until a person is between 30 and 40 years old, by which time many affected people have had children. Most cells in a person's body carry two copies of each gene, but the sex cells, which combine to produce a child, each carry only one copy. In a person who carries the Huntington's disease gene, a given sex cell is equally likely to receive a normal form of the Huntington's gene or the defective form that causes the disease. Although most of the 4,000 or so diseases known to be inherited are caused by recessive genes, the Huntington's gene is dominant, which means that anyone who inherits the gene will eventually develop the illness, even if the person receives a normal gene from the other parent.

Milton Wexler, like his daughter Nancy, was a fighter. In the next few years, besides making sure

A tragedy in her own family spurred Nancy Wexler to guide research that led to the discovery of the gene that causes Huntington's disease, a brain-destroying inherited illness. (Hereditary Disease Foundation. Photo by Rob Marinissen.)

that Leonore was cared for, he learned everything he could about Huntington's disease. He also contacted Marjorie Guthrie, widow of the disease's most famous sufferer, folksinger Woody Guthrie, who wrote and sang "This Land Is Your Land." Guthrie had died of Huntington's in 1967. Soon afterward, Marjorie Guthrie had founded an organization called the Committee to Combat Huntington's Chorea (an older name for the disease, which comes from the Greek word for "dance"). Marjorie Guthrie's organization focused on finding better ways to care for people with Huntington's disease. Milton Wexler, however, was more interested in searching for a cure, so he decided to form his own organization, the Hereditary Disease Foundation. Nancy was a key part of this organization from the time it was founded in 1968. She became the foundation's president in 1983 and still holds this post in 2006.

While Milton Wexler was establishing this new organization, Nancy began a doctoral program in psychology at the University of Michigan, Ann Arbor. (She had earned an A.B. in social relations and English from Radcliffe College in 1967.) Drawing on her own experiences and those of other families with Huntington's whom she interviewed, she wrote her Ph.D. thesis on the mental and emotional effects of being a member of such a family. She received her degree in psychology in 1974.

Needle in a Genetic Haystack

About five times each year, the Hereditary Disease Foundation invites scientists interested in Huntington's research to a combination workshop and dinner. Ideas that might seem too experimental to be brought up at formal scientific gatherings are welcome there.

David Housman of the Massachusetts Institute of Technology (MIT) brought up just such an idea at a meeting in October 1979. He and the other researchers at the workshop knew that the best thing they could do to combat Huntington's would be to identify the gene that caused it. Doing so would produce a test for the disease, which would let people find out whether they carried the dangerous gene. This information might help them decide whether to have children, for instance. Finding the Huntington's gene also could lead

---

CONNECTIONS: AN ILLNESS THAT CHANGED HISTORY

Most inherited diseases bring tragedy only to individual families like Nancy Wexler's. One such disease, however, may have changed history. The disease was hemophilia, which makes its victims bleed and bleed after even the tiniest cut or other injury.

Crown Prince Alexis, the young son of Czar Nicholas of Russia, was born with hemophilia in 1905. No one in those days had heard of genes, but doctors had observed for hundreds of years that this bleeding disease ran in families. One of those families belonged to Queen Victoria, who ruled the United Kingdom for most of the 19th century. The illness was so common among her descendants that some people called it "the royal disease." Alexandra, Nicholas's wife, was one of those descendants. The Russian empress was not sick herself—women almost never developed the disease—but she transmitted the hemophilia gene to her son.

Alexandra was desperate to find a cure for her son's illness, which several times nearly cost him his life. No doctor seemed able to help him. When Alexis was two years old, however, a wild-looking man who called himself Rasputin appeared at the Russian court. He said he was a holy man and could save the crown prince. Wanting to believe him, Alexandra and Nicholas gave him valuable gifts and increasing power in their government.

Rasputin actually could do no more for Alexis than anyone else, and he abused his power in many ways. Russian citizens, nobles and commoners alike, became outraged at the self-proclaimed monk's behavior and the royal couple's insistence on defending him. A number of historians say that anger at Rasputin was one cause of the Russian Revolution, which swept the country in 1917 and cost the royal family not only their throne but their lives.

---

to a better understanding of the illness and, possibly, a treatment or even cure for it.

Finding one gene in the huge human genome seemed far harder than hunting the proverbial needle in a haystack. Scientists had no idea which chromosome the Huntington's gene was on or what protein it made. Still, Housman told the others at the meeting, he had heard of a new technique that might allow the gene to be located.

The technique used restriction enzymes, those same molecular "scissors" that had proven so invaluable in genetic engineering. Molecular biologists had found that, because genes differ slightly in composition from one person to another, a particular restriction enzyme did not snip everyone's DNA into pieces of exactly the same size. A fragment from a certain chromosome in Person A might be 12,000 base pairs long, for instance, while the equivalent fragment from Person B might be 13,500 base pairs long. Researchers had identified a number of spots where these inherited differences appeared. They called them restriction fragment length polymorphisms (*polymorphism* means "something having many forms"), or RFLPs for short. They pronounced this abbreviation "riflips."

Housman explained that RFLPs could be used as markers, like signposts on a road, for other genes that were as yet unknown. If a particular form of RFLP was always or nearly always inherited along with a certain gene, that gene was almost sure to lie very close to the RFLP on a chromosome. If analysis of a person's DNA showed that he or she had inherited the form of the RFLP that was associated with that gene, then the person very probably had inherited the gene as well. (The conclusion could never be completely certain because chromosomes sometimes break when cells reproduce, and a break could fall between the RFLP and the gene and separate the two.)

The problem with looking for the Huntington's gene by studying RFLPs was that no one knew where to start. At the time Housman described the procedure, only one human RFLP marker was known. Skeptics thought it might take 50 years or more to find a RFLP that was linked with the Huntington's gene—if, indeed, such a marker was ever found.

Still, the RFLP idea was better than anything anyone else had thought of. The Hereditary Disease Foundation agreed to provide a grant for Housman's work. Nancy Wexler arranged for further funding through the Congressional Commission for the Control of Huntington's Disease and Its Consequences, of which she had been made executive director in 1976.

Visit to Venezuela

The first thing Housman and his coworkers would need for their research was a large family containing members who had Huntington's disease. The family had to be large because many members, both sick and healthy, would have to be tested in order to establish that a particular form of a RFLP was consistently inherited with the gene that caused the disease. Fortunately, geneticists around the world had begun keeping records of families in which particular inherited diseases occurred. Housman's group learned that the largest American family with Huntington's lived in Iowa. They were also told about a far bigger Huntington's family in Venezuela, on the shores of Lake Maracaibo.

As it happened, Nancy Wexler had known about the Venezuelan family since 1972. Indeed, pursuing a different line of research about the inheritance of the disease, she had visited them earlier in 1979.

It was a remarkable experience. Accompanied by a group of other American and Venezuelan scientists, Wexler had found most members of the family living in three villages: San Luis, Barranquitas, and Laguneta. San Luis was a poverty-stricken settlement on the outskirts of the city of Maracaibo. Barranquitas was in the countryside, several hours' drive away. The third settlement, Laguneta, could be reached only by boat. Wexler and the others found the brightly colored houses in this little fishing village standing on stiltlike pilings above the marshy waters of the lake.

Practically the first person Wexler saw in Laguneta was a skeleton-thin woman hunched in the doorway of one of the stilt houses. When an expedition member spoke to the woman, she spread her arms and began a writhing motion that Wexler recognized all too well. Wexler told Mary Murray, a writer for the *New York Times Magazine,* in 1994,

It was so amazing to me. Here I was in the middle of nowhere, palm trees all around, houses built over the water on stilts. Yet, here was a person who looked exactly like Mom. To be in someplace so

alien and see something so familiar at the same time—that was just breathtaking.

Huntington's disease was so common in this Venezuelan family that family members just accepted it as part of their hard life. They often called the illness *el mal*—"the sickness" or "the bad thing."

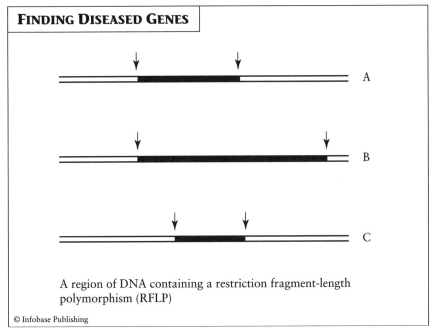

FINDING DISEASED GENES

A region of DNA containing a restriction fragment-length polymorphism (RFLP)

© Infobase Publishing

Researchers can use markers called RFLPs (restriction fragment length polymorphisms) to help them locate a disease-causing gene. Each marker, whose location on a chromosome is known, exists in several forms that can be detected, as shown here. Scientists examine that chromosome in many individuals from a family in which the disease is common. Genes within a chromosome are reshuffled during production of eggs and sperm, but genes that are close together are less likely to be separated by this process than genes that are farther apart. If the researchers find that people who have the disease almost always inherit the same form of a particular RFLP, they conclude that the disease gene is located near that RFLP. Sequencing and other techniques can then be used to determine the disease gene's exact location.

Contrary to the usual experience of families in the United States, even some children had the disease.

Blood, Skin, and DNA

When the RFLP work was ready to start in 1981, Wexler returned to Venezuela to collect blood and skin samples from family members for DNA testing. (Later on, blood alone was used.) At first, the Venezuelans had trouble understanding why Wexler's group wanted these samples, especially why the scientists needed material from seemingly healthy people. Some of the Venezuelan men were also afraid that the sampling procedures would weaken or harm them.

To overcome these fears, the scientists gave a sort of party for the villagers, during which they tried to explain their work. They found that even pointing out that Wexler, like the Venezuelans, was at risk for the disease brought only disbelief. Then, however, Fidela Gómez, an Argentinean nurse with the group, had an inspiration. She lifted Wexler's arm and led her around the room, showing the people the small scar left after Wexler had given her own skin sample. "See, see, see? She has the mark!" Gómez exclaimed. After that, Wexler reported to Lauren Picker, the villagers became very cooperative.

Wexler's team held "draw days" to collect blood samples whenever a member of the team was about to return to the United States. That way, the researcher could carry the samples back. The samples had to reach the laboratory that would analyze them within 48 hours of being collected. They went to Massachusetts General Hospital, where James Gusella, originally a graduate student of Housman's, stored and examined them. Gusella by then was in charge of the Huntington's RFLP project.

By the early 1980s, several dozen human RFLPs had been found. Gusella started by testing for some of them in blood samples from the Iowa family, which were already available. Contrary to the gloomy predictions of scientists who had doubted the new technique, Gusella found some evidence that the 12th RFLP he tried, a marker called G8, was inherited along with the Huntington's gene.

There were not enough members in the American family for him to prove this idea conclusively, however.

Gusella then turned to the samples from the Venezuelans. This time he found that almost all the family members with Huntington's had inherited one form of the G8 marker, while the healthy members had inherited another form. The odds were better than 1,000 to one that this marker was near the Huntington's gene. Gusella and Wexler agreed that he had been amazingly lucky to find the right RFLP so quickly. Gusella and his coworkers, including Wexler and the other members of the Venezuelan team, published their results in *Nature* in November 1983. In addition to providing a vital clue to the location of the Huntington's gene, the group's research showed that tracking RFLPs was a useful technique for finding genes. For the first time, researchers had a hope of locating and identifying particular genes that caused human diseases—the first step toward learning how the genes worked and, perhaps, how to repair or compensate for them.

The most immediate result of Gusella's discovery was the creation of a test that showed with about 96 percent certainty whether a person would develop Huntington's disease. The test began to be used in 1986. Its existence brought Nancy Wexler face to face with a hard personal decision. Did she really want to know whether she would develop the awful disease that by then had killed her mother? How would she feel, and what would she do, if she found she had the gene? She had already decided not to have children, so she did not need to know for that reason. Maintaining her right to privacy, Wexler has consistently refused to say whether she has taken the Huntington's test, let alone what the results might have been. If she has decided not to use the test, however, she is far from alone. In the decade after the test came into use, only 13 percent of Americans at risk for the disease chose to be tested.

Gene Hunters Find Their Prey

Once they found the RFLP marker, Gusella and the other genetic researchers began their next quest: the search for the Huntington's gene itself. Only if the gene was located could they sequence it, identify its protein, and begin to learn how this bit of DNA produced its deadly effects. To speed the hunt, in 1984 the Hereditary Disease

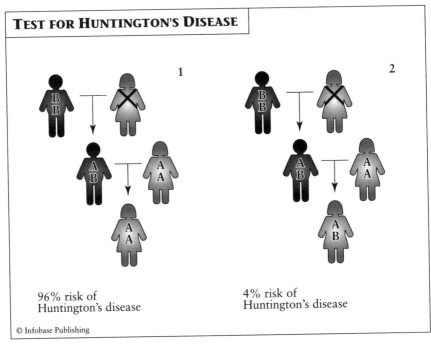

TEST FOR HUNTINGTON'S DISEASE

96% risk of
Huntington's disease

4% risk of
Huntington's disease

© Infobase Publishing

The first test for Huntington's disease used a RFLP marker to stand in for the disease gene, which at that time was still unknown. People could inherit several different forms of the marker (shown here as A, B, and C). In this example, a woman (bottom row) who has inherited the A form of the marker from both parents wants to know whether she will develop the disease. Her father (male figure, middle row) has Huntington's disease; her mother (female figure, middle row) is healthy. The father's father (male figure, top row) carries only form B of the marker and does not have Huntington's. The father's mother (female figure, top row) is dead, so the type of marker she carried is unknown (X). In the father's family, the A form of the marker must be associated with the Huntington's gene. The woman has inherited one of her A markers from her father, so she has a 96 percent chance of developing the disease. If she had inherited a B marker from him, she would have had only a 4 percent risk of the disease. (Her mother's A marker is not associated with a Huntington's gene because no one in the mother's family has a disease-causing form of that gene.)

Foundation persuaded research groups at six institutions in the United States and Britain to collaborate on the work. The groups agreed not only to share their research results but to sign scientific papers only

---

SOCIAL IMPACT: GENETIC DISCRIMINATION

Nancy Wexler says that people should be allowed to be tested for genes like the one that causes Huntington's disease if they wish to be. Such tests can help people plan their future or decide whether to have children. However, she also warns that testing can be dangerous. If the disease being tested for is incurable, like Huntington's, people who learn that they have the disease gene may feel depressed or even consider killing themselves. Genetic testing should never be given without extensive counseling both before and after the test, Wexler says.

As testing for genes that cause or contribute to disease becomes more common, Wexler fears that another problem may develop. People who have genes associated with increased risk of, say, heart disease or cancer may find themselves unable to find a life partner, a home, or a job. Many health insurance policies do not cover the cost of treating "preexisting conditions"—medical problems that a person has when the policy is taken out. Insurers may consider genetic predispositions to disease to be preexisting conditions, even if a person is not sick and may never develop the disease. Since most large businesses provide health insurance for their employees, companies may be reluctant to hire people with health problems or even the likelihood of developing such problems.

In a few decades, information from the Human Genome Project may allow a person's entire genetic heritage to be read at birth. Helpful as such a gene profile might be in some ways, Wexler thinks it could greatly increase the chances of discrimination based on a person's genes. "All of us have something or other in our genes that's going to get us in trouble," Wexler told Lauren Picker in 1994. "We'll all be uninsurable." From 1989 to 1995, because of Wexler's concern about genetic discrimination and related problems arising from the Human Genome Project, she was chosen to head a committee that oversaw research on the ethical, legal, and social issues raised by the project.

with their collective name, the Huntington's Disease Collaborative Research Group.

Such cooperation was almost unheard of, especially in the highly competitive field that genetics had become. Inevitably, the collaboration did not always go smoothly. The researchers involved agree that Nancy Wexler was the glue that held it together. She went from laboratory to laboratory, encouraging the scientists and calming conflicts between them. Despite the research group's best efforts, however, the Huntington's gene remained elusive throughout the 1980s. By 1984, the group had learned that the marker RFLP, and therefore the disease gene, was on the short arm of chromosome 4. The Huntington's gene was the first to be mapped to a particular chromosome through RFLP markers alone. Beyond that, though, the group's luck seemed to have run out.

The gene hunters finally found their quarry early in 1993. Marcy MacDonald, a senior researcher working with James Gusella, then sequenced the Huntington's gene—and learned what was wrong with it. Near the gene's beginning she found a sort of molecular stutter, a repeating sequence of the bases C-A-G (cytosine-adenine-guanine). This group of bases is the genetic code "letter" that stands for glutamine, an amino acid that sometimes harms nerve cells, and extra copies of this sequence meant that the gene's protein would contain extra glutamine. The genes of people unaffected by the disease had between 11 and 34 C-A-G repeats. In people who developed Huntington's, however, the repeats numbered 40 or more—sometimes up to 125. (People with 35 to 39 repeats sometimes became ill and sometimes did not.) The more repeats an affected person's gene had, researchers eventually learned, the sooner in life the disease would appear and the more severe it would be. Some Venezuelan family members became sick when they were as young as two years old, whereas, at the other extreme, the disease could be delayed until a person was 84.

Scientists have identified the Huntington gene's protein, which they call huntingtin. The protein's exact function is still unknown, but it seems to affect the way cells make energy. The mutation in the disease gene appears to make strands of the protein form clumps, or aggregates, inside neurons, which may damage the cells.

OTHER SCIENTISTS: MARY-CLAIRE KING (1946–   )

Huntington's disease, like most inherited diseases caused by a single gene, is rare. However, genes also contribute to more common diseases, such as cancer and heart disease. Inheriting a particular form of certain genes can increase the chances that someone will develop one of these illnesses.

In 1974, even before the hunt for the Huntington's gene began, Mary-Claire King, a geneticist then working at the University of California, Berkeley, set out to prove that genes could increase a woman's risk of developing breast cancer. At the time, only a few rare cancers were known to be inherited, and most cancer researchers doubted that heredity played any part in more common forms of the disease. However, King, born on February 27, 1946, had noticed that some families contained unusually large numbers of breast cancer victims, and women from these families developed the disease at a much earlier age than other women did. To her, this suggested inheritance.

King eventually proved that about 5 percent of breast cancers are inherited. Using some of the same marker techniques that Nancy Wexler's group applied, King's research team determined in 1990 that a probable breast cancer gene lay halfway down the lower arm of chromosome 17. Mark Skolnick of the University of Utah Medical Center identified the gene itself, called BRCA1, in 1994, a year after the Huntington's gene was found.

King, now at the University of Washington in Seattle, has also traced the heredity of other conditions, including inherited deafness. In addition, she has used her gene-tracking techniques to reunite children and grandparents separated by war and to map the migration of human populations.

Immeasurable Love

While the search for the gene that causes Huntington's disease was going on, Nancy Wexler pursued the illness from a different angle by continuing her yearly visits to the Venezuelan family, whom

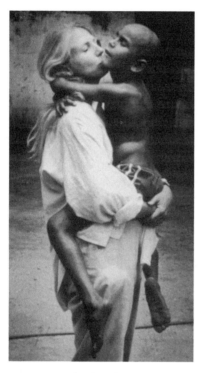

Nancy Wexler has been said to give "immeasurable love" to members of the large Venezuelan family she studies, such as this child with Huntington's disease. (Hereditary Disease Foundation. Photo by Peter Ginter)

she now regarded as almost her own flesh and blood. In addition to collecting more blood samples, she and her group enlarged their knowledge of the villagers' family tree. Today, part of their genealogy diagram covers the walls of the corridor outside Wexler's office at the Columbia University Medical Center, where she has been a professor since 1984. (Before that, she was a health science administrator at the National Institute of Neurological Diseases and Stroke, part of the National Institutes of Health.) She is currently Higgins Professor of Neurology at the university's medical school and is also on the faculty of the Columbia Center for Bioethics.

The Venezuelan family tree now includes 10 generations, totaling more than 18,000 people. According to a March 2004 press release from Columbia, the Venezuelans make up the world's largest genetically related community that carries the Huntington's gene. Wexler and her coworkers have established that most of them are descended from one woman, Maria Concepción Soto, who lived in the area in the early 19th century. "From this one woman," Walter Bodmer and Robin McKie quoted Wexler as saying in their book about recent discoveries in human genetics, *The Book of Man,* "a huge pyramid of suffering has been stretching out over the decades."

Besides studying the Venezuelan family's genealogy, Wexler and the others on her team also care for the family as best they can.

Américo Negrette, the Venezuelan doctor who first discovered the family, wrote in a Venezuelan magazine quoted in Robert Cook-Deegan's book about the Human Genome Project, *Gene Wars,* that Wexler

> *brings them [the villagers] medicines and . . . projects for their social welfare. . . . She [also] brings them an immeasurable love. . . . I have seen her embracing women and embracing men and kissing children. Without theatre, without simulation, without pose. With a tenderness that jumps from her eyes.*

Awards Wexler has received, such as the Albert Lasker Public Service Award (1993) and the J. Allyn Taylor International Prize in Medicine (1994), honor this love as well as Wexler's sponsorship of groundbreaking research into the causes of inherited disease.

Wexler's study of the Venezuelan family still continues. In March 2004, for example, her research led her to report that the number of C-A-G repeats in the Huntington's gene is not the only factor that affects the age at which family members begin to show signs of the disease. The influence of certain other genes and environmental factors can delay the illness's onset, she believes. If researchers can learn more about these delaying factors, she says, physicians might become able to postpone illness in people who inherit the defective Huntington's gene or even keep them from developing the disease at all. Wexler hopes that, if this day comes, the Venezuelan families will be restored to health. "The Venezuelan families have given us many gifts," a Columbia press release quoted her as saying. "It would be fitting if they could be the first to reap the benefits of all future therapies."

Chronology

1872	George Huntington describes Huntington's disease
1945	Nancy Wexler born in Washington, D.C., on July 19
1967	Folksinger Woody Guthrie dies of Huntington's

1968	Nancy Wexler learns that her mother has Huntington's
	Milton and Nancy Wexler establish Hereditary Disease Foundation to support research on Huntington's disease and related disorders
1972	Nancy Wexler learns about large Venezuelan family in whom Huntington's disease is common
1974	Nancy Wexler receives Ph.D. in psychology from University of Michigan, Ann Arbor
1976	Nancy Wexler chosen to head Congressional Commission for the Control of Huntington's Disease and Its Consequences
1979	Nancy Wexler visits family with Huntington's in Venezuela for first time
	In October, David Housman proposes looking for Huntington's gene by using restriction fragment length polymorphisms (RFLPs)
1981	RFLP work starts
	Nancy Wexler's research group collects first genetic samples from Venezuelan family
1983	James Gusella discovers RFLP marker for Huntington's gene
1984	Huntington's Disease Collaborative Research Group formed Huntington's Research Group discovers that Huntington's gene is near end of short arm of chromosome 4
	Nancy Wexler joins faculty of Columbia University
1986	Test for Huntington's marker first used
1989	Nancy Wexler chosen to head committee researching the ethical, legal, and social implications of Human Genome Project
1993	Researchers locate Huntington's disease gene and identify its defect
	Nancy Wexler receives Albert Lasker Public Service Award
2004	Nancy Wexler shows that certain genes and environmental factors can delay the onset of Huntington's disease

Further Reading

Books

Bodmer, Walter, and Robin McKie. *The Book of Man.* New York: Scribner, 1994.
> Describes recent discoveries about human genetics, including the finding of the Huntington's disease gene.

Cook-Deegan, Robert. *The Gene Wars: Science, Politics, and the Human Genome.* New York: W. W. Norton, 1994.
> Discusses scientific and political conflicts during the early stages of the Human Genome Project and the ethical issues this research raises, including the risk of genetic discrimination.

Glimm, Adele. *Gene Hunter: The Story of Neuropsychologist Nancy Wexler.* Danbury, Conn.: Franklin Watts, 2005.
> Biography of Wexler for young adults.

Wexler, Alice. *Mapping Fate.* New York: Random House/Times Books, 1995.
> Memoir written by Nancy Wexler's older sister describes the loss of their mother to Huntington's disease and the medical research to locate the disease-causing gene that Nancy Wexler and her father, Milton, sponsored.

Wexler, Nancy. "Clairvoyance and Caution: Repercussions from the Human Genome Project." In *The Code of Codes,* edited by Daniel J. Kevles and Leroy Hood. Cambridge, Mass.: Harvard University Press, 1992.
> Long essay by Wexler describes the search for the Huntington's gene and considers the ethical and social issues raised by genetic testing.

Articles

Gusella, J. F., et al. "A Polymorphic DNA Marker Genetically Linked to Huntington's Disease," *Nature,* 17 November 1983, pp. 234–238.
> Scientific paper reporting location of a RFLP marker usually inherited with the gene that causes Huntington's disease.

Huntington's Disease Collaborative Research Group. "A Novel Gene Containing a Trinucleotide Repeat That Is Expanded

and Unstable on Huntington's Disease Chromosomes," *Cell* 72 (March 26, 1993): 971–983.
Scientific paper describing location of the gene that causes Huntington's disease and identification of the gene's defect.

Murray, Mary. "Nancy Wexler," *New York Times Magazine,* 13 February 1994, p. 28.
Extensive article on Wexler and her work, written soon after the discovery of the Huntington's gene.

Picker, Lauren. "All in the Family," *American Health,* 13 (March 1994): 20–23.
Profile of Wexler and description of her research.

"A Tale of Pain and Hope on Lake Maracaibo," *Business Week,* 5 June 2000, pp. 20E/O.
Describes Wexler's research on a large Venezuelan family in which Huntington's disease is common.

"Venezuelan Kindreds Reveal Genetic and Environmental Factors Influence Onset of Huntington's Disease." Columbia University Medical Center press release. March 2, 2004. Available online. URL: http://www.hdfoundation.org/news/20040302-CUMC.htm. Accessed on November 12, 2004.
Describes research by Nancy Wexler showing that certain factors can delay the onset of Huntington's disease.

"Wexler, Nancy S." *Current Biography Yearbook 1994,* 607–611. New York: H. W. Wilson, 1994.
Profile of Wexler, written soon after the discovery of the Huntington's gene, summarizes other material written about her.

Web Sites

Hereditary Disease Foundation. This organization, founded by Nancy Wexler and her father, Milton, in 1968, sponsors research on Huntington's disease and related disorders. Their site includes news briefs on recent discoveries about the disease and possible treatments for it. www.hdfoundation.org. Accessed on January 6, 2005.

6

THE LIVE-FOREVER WORM

CYNTHIA KENYON AND THE GENETICS OF AGING

About 500 years ago, the Indians of what is now Puerto Rico told Spanish explorer Juan Ponce de León a wild story about a magic fountain. Whoever drank from its waters, they said, would stay young forever. Intrigued, de León sailed off to look for the fountain in 1513. He eventually discovered Florida, but he never found the Fountain of Youth.

San Francisco biochemist Cynthia Kenyon thinks she may have succeeded where the deluded de León failed. The trail to the Fountain of Youth, she claims, lies not through tropical swamps but through the genes of a worm almost too small to see.

New Career Path

Cynthia Kenyon never planned to be either an explorer or a biologist. Born in Chicago on February 18, 1954, she thought first of being a musician (she loved the French horn) or, later, when she entered the University of Georgia at Athens, a writer. Both of Kenyon's parents had academic backgrounds—her father was a professor of geography at the university, and her mother was an administrator in its physics department—but Kenyon's own university experiences were not happy at first. Unsure what to do with her life, she dropped out before earning a degree.

Cynthia Kenyon's research on worms may provide a way to slow down human aging. (Cynthia Kenyon)

While Kenyon was still thinking about her future, her mother happened one day to bring home a book called *Molecular Biology of the Gene,* written by James Watson, the codiscoverer of DNA. "I thought: This is really cool, you know, genes getting switched on and off," Kenyon recalled in a 2004 interview with David Ewing Duncan. Her excitement about Watson's book turned her career deliberations in a new direction. She went back to the University of Georgia and, this time, studied biochemistry. Kenyon graduated in 1976 as valedictorian of her class.

A Valuable Worm

Kenyon did her graduate work at the Massachusetts Institute of Technology (MIT), studying the way DNA-damaging chemicals affect bacteria. When she visited the laboratory next door, scientist Bob Horvitz introduced her to his own research animal: a tiny worm whose scientific name, *Caenorhabditis elegans,* was far larger than the worm itself. A single *C. elegans* is only 0.04 inch (1 mm) long, about as big as the period at the end of this sentence.

C. elegans is a type of worm called a nematode, or roundworm. According to journalist Andrew Brown's book about research on *C. elegans, In the Beginning Was the Worm,* nematodes "are overwhelmingly the most numerous animals on Earth." They are also among the planet's oldest multicelled creatures. Some nematodes are parasites, living on or in a variety of other living things, including humans, but *C. elegans* lives harmlessly in soil or compost heaps and eats mostly bacteria. The worm has a smooth, cylindrical body that tapers to a point at each end.

In the early 1960s, when Cynthia Kenyon was still a child, Sydney Brenner, a South African–born biologist, began research that eventually made this unassuming worm one of laboratory biology's best-known test animals. Brenner and others who followed him found that *C. elegans* had many advantages for scientists. To begin with, the worms could be raised easily in petri dishes containing a jelly packed with their favorite bacterial food. The nematodes multiplied almost as fast as the bacteria they ate, each worm producing a new generation of 300 or so every three days. Under most conditions, a single *C. elegans* made male as well as female sex cells and mated with itself, which meant that any genetic mutation arising in a worm would appear repeatedly in its offspring. Each worm had only about 1,000 cells, but that small number included all the cell types found in humans and other mammals. Finally, being almost transparent, the nematodes were perfect for studying under a microscope. Andrew Brown calls *C. elegans* "nature's test tube." According to Brown, Sydney Brenner himself claimed that "With a few toothpicks [to pick up the worms], some petri dishes, and a microscope, you can open the door to all of biology."

Focus on Aging

Kenyon found Horvitz's roundworms fascinating because their development could be traced cell by cell, and she decided that she would

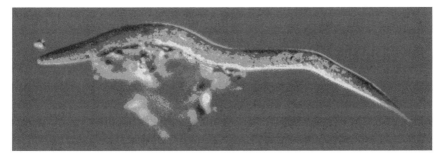

This tiny roundworm, Caenorhabditis elegans, *lives in soil and eats bacteria. Scientists have studied its genes extensively, uncovering important information about development and aging.* (Maria E. Gallegos)

OTHER SCIENTISTS: SYDNEY BRENNER (1927–)

Sydney Brenner was born in 1927 near Johannesburg, South Africa, to Jewish parents who had emigrated from eastern Europe. He worked with Francis Crick at Cambridge University in the late 1950s and early 1960s to discover how cells use the "genetic code" in DNA molecules to construct proteins. Brenner then turned to researching the way genes influenced animals' development before birth, using *C. elegans* as his test subject.

During the next two decades, Brenner, his coworkers, and other laboratories inspired by him worked out the worm's development, cell by cell. By studying mutations, they determined which genes guided cells to certain places in the worm's body, which genes told cells to mature into different types such as nerve or muscle, and which genes told cells to die. The researchers located these genes on the nematode's chromosomes and worked out the sequence of bases in some of them, a process that at the time was extremely tedious and time-consuming. According to Andrew Brown's history of *C. elegans* research, the body of knowledge about this tiny worm that Brenner and his followers accumulated was the inspiration for similarly detailed studies of other multicelled creatures and eventually led to the Human Genome Project. In 1998, *C. elegans* became the first multicelled organism to have its complete genome sequenced.

Sydney Brenner won a share of the Nobel Prize in physiology or medicine in 2002 for his work on the way genes orchestrate an organism's development. He shared the prize with John Sulston and Bob Horvitz, the scientist who introduced Cynthia Kenyon to *C. elegans*.

rather study them than bacteria. After she finished her Ph.D. work in 1981, her interest in the worms took her to Cambridge to work under Sydney Brenner. She spent five years there studying how the nematodes developed before birth, and then returned to the United States and joined the University of California, San Francisco (UCSF), in 1986 as an assistant professor. She became a full professor of biochemistry and biophysics in 1992.

The focus of Kenyon's studies changed around 1990, when she happened to pick up a petri dish that she had meant to discard a month earlier. The dish contained mutant worms that did not reproduce well, so it was not as crowded as such dishes normally would be. Most of the worms left in it were old, nearing the end of their 20-day lifespan. "I had never seen an old worm. I had never even thought about an old

---

PARALLELS: THE DISCOVERY OF PENICILLIN

Cynthia Kenyon was not the first scientist whose career was changed by a forgotten laboratory dish. In 1928, the Scottish bacteriologist Alexander Fleming, showing a friend around his London laboratory, passed a stack of petri dishes that had gone uncleaned while Fleming was on a recent vacation. According to Gwyn Macfarlane's biography *Alexander Fleming: The Man and the Myth*, Fleming picked up one dish, looked at it hard, and said to his friend, "That's funny." The dishes contained colonies of staphylococci, a type of bacteria that infects wounds. Fleming noticed that a speck of mold, or fungus, similar to the blue mold that sometimes grows on stale bread, had landed on this dish—and around the mold was a clear area, showing that no bacteria grew there.

Fleming went on to study the mold that had "spoiled" his culture dish and the bacteria-killing substance that the fungus produced. The mold belonged to a group called *Penicillium,* so he called the "mold juice" penicillin. Fleming published a paper on the mold and its chemical in 1929, but he did not pursue his research for long after that. He concluded that penicillin would be worthless in medicine because he could not purify it, and in impure form it lost its effectiveness quickly. Ten years later, however, two Oxford University scientists, the Australian-born pathologist Howard Florey and Ernst Chain, a biochemist who had recently fled Nazi Germany, read Fleming's paper and decided to reinvestigate penicillin. Using improved techniques, Chain purified the germ-killing part of the "mold juice," and Florey's research group showed that the purified substance could stop the growth of dangerous bacteria in the bodies of mice and humans. American drug companies built on the Oxford team's work to mass-produce penicillin in the early 1940s. As the first antibiotic to be widely used, penicillin saved millions of lives in World War II and revolutionized the treatment of infectious diseases.

worm," Kenyon later told *U.S. News & World Report* writer Nell Boyce. Nonetheless, the young scientist had no trouble recognizing these nematode senior citizens: They were shrunken and wrinkled, and they moved much less vigorously than young worms. "I felt sorry for them," Kenyon said to Boyce. They reminded her that she was growing older, too, she told the reporter. "And right on the heels of that [thought], I thought, 'Oh, my gosh, you could study this.'"

Conducting a Genetic Orchestra

Kenyon began looking at mutant *C. elegans* worms, discovered by other scientists, that lived longer than normal. She tried altering genes in her worms in the hope of reproducing the mutations' effects. Finally, in 1993, she and her coworkers showed that worms with modifications in genes called daf-2 and daf-16 lived twice as long as normal nematodes. Furthermore, the ancient animals appeared much healthier and more vigorous than old worms usually did. "It's like you're looking at someone who is 90 and you think they're 45," Kenyon explained to Steven Kotler, an interviewer for *Discover* magazine, in 2004.

Researchers were amazed when Kenyon announced that changes in just two genes could postpone aging, even in a worm. Many scientists at the time believed that aging was the result of damage to cells and tissues that built up during a lifetime of use: Essentially, bodies simply wore out. Other researchers thought, instead, that evolution had programmed aging and death into living things to keep organisms from wasting resources after they had stopped reproducing and therefore were no longer biologically useful. Almost no one believed that aging was directly controlled by genes or that anything could be done to extend lifespan or stop the breakdowns and diseases that usually accompany growing old. Kenyon, however, pointed out that bats, for example, can live for 50 years, whereas mice, which are also mammals and are about the same size as small bats, usually live for only two years. She insisted that genes could explain such differences. (Not all scientists agree. S. J. Olshansky of the University of Illinois at Chicago, for instance, told *Smithsonian* writer Stephen S. Hall, "There are no death or aging genes—period.")

Aging, whether in worms or humans, involves many different changes, so it seemed clear that daf-2 and daf-16 must be "master genes" that control the activity of numerous other genes. Kenyon and others have since learned that the two controlling genes affect perhaps as many as 100 others between them. "You can think of daf-2

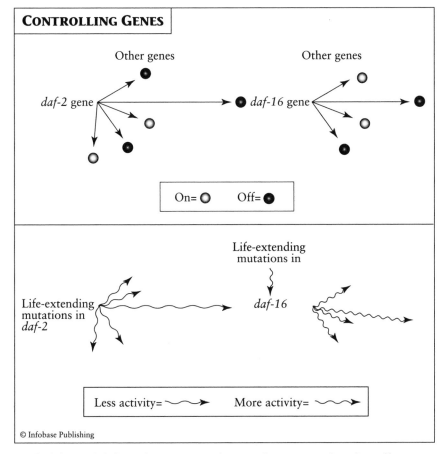

© Infobase Publishing

Both daf-2 and daf-16, the two genes that Cynthia Kenyon found to affect lifespan in nematodes, turn many other genes on and off. They also oppose each other, so when daf-2 is active, it blocks much of the activity of daf-16. Mutations that extend life in the worms make daf-2 less active, whereas life-extending mutations in daf-16 make the gene more active.

as the orchestra conductor leading the flutes and the violins and the cellos, each doing a little bit," Kenyon said to David Duncan. The two master genes seemed to oppose each other, Kenyon reported: the life-extending change in daf-2 made that gene less active, while the mutation in daf-16 increased the gene's activity. Kenyon later termed daf-2 the "grim reaper" gene and daf-16 the "Fountain of Youth" gene. She thinks that both master genes appeared very early in evolution, when the first living things were struggling to survive

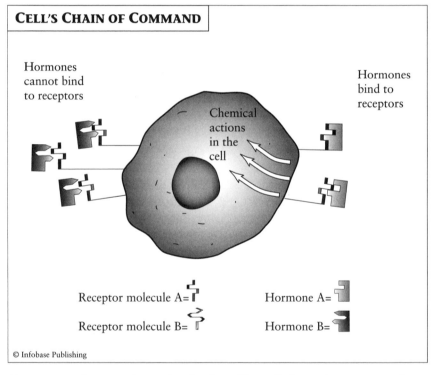

CELL'S CHAIN OF COMMAND

Hormones cannot bind to receptors

Hormones bind to receptors

Chemical actions in the cell

Receptor molecule A=

Receptor molecule B=

Hormone A=

Hormone B=

© Infobase Publishing

Hormones and many other molecules that affect cells begin their activity when they attach, or bind, to receptor molecules on the surface of the cells. Genes such as daf-2 in nematodes carry the code to make these receptors, which are proteins. Each receptor is shaped to fit a particular substance, as the mechanism in a lock fits with a particular key. When a hormone binds to a receptor, a cascade of chemical events within the cell is triggered. These events may make the cell grow and divide, for instance.

the storms, harsh solar radiation, and volcanic eruptions that made the early Earth a terrifying place.

By 2003, Kenyon and others had discovered more than 30 other genes that, guided by the master genes, help to extend lifespan. The researchers are trying to learn, in effect, what instruments these individual members of the genetic orchestra play and how they contribute to the symphony of extended life. Some genes, Kenyon says, prevent damage to cells and genes caused by heat or chemicals called free radicals, which pile up in cells as living things age. Other genes repair damaged proteins or change the way the body uses food and energy. Still others fight off illnesses caused by bacteria.

Genes and Hormones

Kenyon's discovery sparked other scientists' interest in aging's relationship to genes. Some laboratories began looking for genes similar to daf-2 and daf-16 in animals besides nematodes, and they found them in creatures ranging from yeast (a fungus) to mice. Others tried to learn exactly what these genes do in the body. They discovered that daf-2 makes a protein, found on the surface of certain cells in the worm, that acts as a receptor for a particular kind of hormone.

Hormones are substances made in one part of the body that affect the action of other parts. Some hormones produce growth, for instance, while others control sexual development and reproduction. These chemicals can act only on cells that have receptors for them. A hormone molecule fits into its receptor like a key fitting into the lock of a door. When the two join together, they "unlock" genes within the cell and set off a complex series of physical and chemical changes. Daf-16 also turns genes on and off, but by a different mechanism.

Gary Ruvkun, a scientist at Harvard Medical School, showed in 1997 that the hormone for which daf-2 makes the receptor is related to two other hormones that exist in mammals, including humans. One is insulin, which controls the way the body uses food. The second substance, which is similar to insulin in some ways, is called insulinlike growth factor 1. As its name suggests, this protein makes cells grow and divide.

Ruvkun's discovery suggested that changes in genes similar to daf-2 and daf-16 might affect aging in humans as well as worms. In early 2003, Ron Kahn at Harvard Medical School and, independently, Martin Holzenberger at the French Biomedical Research Agency reported further evidence for this idea. When they inactivated daf-2-like genes in mice, the mice lived 26 percent longer than normal mice. Like Kenyon's worms, the mice also remained young-looking and apparently healthy throughout their lives.

Low Calories, Long Life

Some researchers are investigating the relationship between these genes and hormones and the one other treatment that has been shown to extend lifespan: a semistarvation diet. Since insulin affects an organism's use of food, such a connection would not be surprising. In the 1930s, Clive M. McCay, a Cornell University scientist, fed rats diets high in nutrients but very low in calories, a treatment later found to lower insulin levels sharply. He found that the half-starved rodents lived 20 to 40 percent longer than rats given a normal diet. Later scientists found similar effects in creatures ranging from yeast and fruit flies to fish.

A few individuals have also tried to extend their lives by eating carefully balanced, low-calorie diets. Science has not proved whether this approach really works, however, and most people probably would not want to adopt it even if it did. Some scientists think that eventually a drug or gene therapy will provide the benefits of a low-calorie diet without its unpleasantness. Alternatively, some nutritionists think that lowering the amount of carbohydrates in the diet will work as well as reducing calories. Carbohydrates, especially those in sugar and foods that are easily converted into sugar, such as candy, potatoes, pasta, and rice, raise the amount of insulin in the blood and affect the way cells react to this hormone. (Other carbohydrates, such as those in beans and whole grains, produce a much smaller increase in insulin.) Low-carbohydrate diets are popular today, and some nutritionists believe that such diets, even when they are not low in calories, can make people healthier as well as helping them lose weight. Cynthia Kenyon herself eats a diet low in easily converted carbohydrates.

Search for Antiaging Drugs

Cynthia Kenyon, meanwhile, continues to manipulate genes in her nematodes. In October 2004, she announced that she had created worms that live up to 125 days—six times their normal lifespan. A human given an equally effective treatment would live to be more than 400 years old. Instead of pitying the animals, as she pitied the first elderly worms she saw, Kenyon says she envies them. She told Nell Boyce, "I wanted to be those worms."

Kenyon's work on the genetics of aging has brought her widespread fame. In 1997, UCSF made her the Herbert Boyer Distinguished Professor of Biochemistry and Biophysics. She also heads the university's Hillblom Center for the Biology of Aging and was elected president of the Genetics Society of America in 2003. She won an award from the Ellison Medical Foundation in 1998 and the King Faisal International Prize for Medicine in 2000. The Faisal Prize included a $200,000 cash award.

Although altered genes have made Cynthia Kenyon's worms live longer, she does not believe that gene therapy is the best way to extend the length of human life. Instead, she thinks scientists can create drugs that imitate the effects of changed genes by altering production of hormones or their receptors. In 2000, she cofounded a company called Elixir Pharmaceuticals in Cambridge, Massachusetts, that is trying to develop such drugs. The company is already testing some drugs in mice. Kenyon's first goal for these drugs is to delay or prevent crippling diseases associated with aging, such as heart disease, many kinds of cancer, and Alzheimer's disease, which damages the brain, destroying the power to think and remember.

The Real Fountain of Youth

Cynthia Kenyon says that her most important discovery is that aging is not completely unavoidable. Instead, "we begin to think of aging as a disease that can be cured, or at least postponed," she and another Elixir cofounder, Leonard Guarente, wrote in an article quoted by *Smithsonian* writer Stephen Hall. Lifespan, Kenyon says, is determined by the result of competition between

SOCIAL IMPACT: THE DANGERS OF EXTENDING LIFE

Few people would object to a treatment that prevents heart attacks or Alzheimer's disease, but critics such as conservative ethicist Leon Kass have questioned whether greatly extending overall human life-span is a good idea. Earth is already overpopulated, these opponents of life extension point out. They claim that adding large numbers of older people, many of whom might need expensive medical care, could produce financial and ecological disaster. At very least, a high proportion of life-extended people might produce an excessively conservative society, eminent Harvard zoologist Edward O. Wilson wrote in *Esquire* in May 1999. Such people "would have the physical capabilities of teenagers but . . . [would be] culturally, educationally, and emotionally aged. . . . Those who have survived and enjoyed longevity extension . . . won't be revolutionaries. They won't be bold entrepreneurs or explorers who risk their lives."

Cynthia Kenyon, however, thinks that antiaging treatments will develop slowly enough for society to have time to adjust to them. "If everyone ages twice as slowly, you'll still have the same percentage of old and young. So we're not talking about filling up the world with old and infirm people," she told David Duncan. On the contrary, she says, life-extended people would continue working and would be active contributors to society. The overpopulation problem, Kenyon says, can be solved by lowering the birth rate—encouraging people to have fewer children and have them later in life. "With a life-span-extending pill, the birthrate would have to come down just a little more" than it needs to do already, she thinks.

two sets of forces, those that break down or damage cells and those that preserve, maintain, and repair them. "In most animals, the force of destruction still has the edge. But why not bump up the genes just a little bit, the maintenance genes?" she asked David Duncan.

In the far future, Kenyon believes, people may be able to take a pill that really accomplishes what the Indians promised Ponce de León that the waters of the magic fountain would do: grant, if not immortality and eternal youth, something very close. Would she herself want to live to be, say, 150 years old? "Of course," she told David Duncan in 2004, "if I'm young and healthy. Wouldn't everyone?"

Chronology

1930s	Cornell University researcher Clive M. McCay shows that rats fed a nutritionally balanced diet very low in calories live 20 to 40 percent longer than normal rats
1954	Cynthia Kenyon born in Chicago on February 18
1960s	Early in the decade, Sydney Brenner begins genetic research on nematode worms at Cambridge University
1981	Kenyon earns Ph.D. from MIT and decides to study worm development under Brenner
1986	Kenyon joins University of California, San Francisco (UCSF)
1990	Kenyon begins research on aging
1993	Kenyon shows that changes in two genes make worms live twice as long as normal
1997	Gary Ruvkun shows that daf-2 gene makes a receptor for a hormone similar to insulin
	UCSF names Kenyon the Herbert Boyer Distinguished Professor of Biochemistry and Biophysics
1998	*Caenorhabditis elegans* genome sequenced
1999	Kenyon cofounds Elixir, a Massachusetts company that is trying to develop antiaging drugs
2000	Kenyon wins King Faisal International Prize for Medicine
2003	Two groups of scientists report extending lives of mice by altering a gene similar to daf-2
	Kenyon produces worms that live six times as long as normal and are healthy and active

Further Reading

Books

Brown, Andrew. *In the Beginning Was the Worm.* New York: Columbia University Press, 2003.
> Describes history of research on *Caenorhabditis elegans,* especially that of Sydney Brenner and his coworkers.

Hall, Stephen S. *Merchants of Immortality.* Boston: Houghton Mifflin, 2003.
> Describes scientists and entrepreneurs who are trying to slow or stop aging and extend life.

Macfarlane, Gwyn. *Alexander Fleming: The Man and the Myth.* Cambridge, Mass.: Harvard University Press, 1984. Biography of Fleming corrects misconceptions about him.

Articles

Block, Melissa. "Discovering the Genetic Controls That Dictate Life Span." *LE Magazine,* June 2002. Available online. URL: http://www.lef.org/magazine/mag2002/jun2002_report_kenyon_01.html. Accessed on September 15, 2004.
> Describes the antiaging research of Cynthia Kenyon and her laboratory.

Boyce, Nell. "In a Hurry to Slow Life's Clock." *U.S. News & World Report,* 29 December 2003, p. 74.
> Short article on Kenyon and her discoveries.

Duncan, David Ewing. "The Biologist Who Extends Life Spans." *Discover,* March 2004, pp. 16–18.
> Extensive interview with Kenyon.

Fleming, Alexander. "On the Antibacterial Action of Cultures of a *Penicillium,* with Special Reference to Their Use in the Isolation of *B. influenzae.*" *British Journal of Experimental Pathology* 10 (1929): 226–236.
> Scientific paper describing Fleming's discovery of penicillin.

Hall, Stephen S. "Kenyon's Ageless Quest," *Smithsonian,* March 2004, pp. 56–63.
> Detailed article on Kenyon and her discoveries, including related research by other laboratories.

Kenyon, C. J., et al. "A *C. elegans* Mutant That Lives Twice as Long as Wild Type," *Nature,* 2 December 1993, pp. 461–464.
   Scientific paper describing Kenyon's discovery of a mutant form of the nematode worm *Caenorhabditis elegans* that had an extended lifespan.
"Kenyon, Cynthia." In *Current Biography Yearbook 2005.* New York: H. W. Wilson, 2005.
   Biographical profile of Kenyon, with quotes from interviews.
Kotler, Steven. "Cynthia Kenyon," *Discover,* November 2004, p. 78.
   Short interview with Kenyon.
Wilson, Edward O. "A World of Immortal Men," *Esquire,* May 1999, p. 84.
   Opinion piece by eminent zoologist questioning whether lifespan extension would benefit society.

7

HELLO, DOLLY

IAN WILMUT AND CLONING

When a lamb is born, usually only its mother and perhaps the farmer who owns it knows or cares. The birth of a lamb named Dolly, however, was featured on the front page of the *New York Times* on February 23, 1997. In the months that followed, speakers and writers poured out millions of impassioned words about this ordinary-looking sheep. Some people even said that Dolly's birth could change the meaning of being human.

Dolly caused all this excitement because she was a clone, an exact genetic copy of another animal. She was not the first animal, or even the first mammal, to be cloned. She was, however, the first animal to be cloned from a mature cell of an adult animal. To scientists, this meant that the clock of a cell's development could be turned back, a feat no one had dreamed was possible. To most people, though, Dolly's birth meant that the creation of a human clone—a baby who would be a genetic duplicate of an existing adult—was only a matter of time.

Ian Wilmut, the leader of the team who created Dolly at a quiet agricultural research laboratory in Scotland, did not want to clone people. He did not even set out to clone animals. The road that led to Dolly was a long one, with many twists and turns.

Sailor to Farmer to Scientist

Ian Wilmut's first plan was to be a sailor. He was born in Hampton Lucy, England, on July 7, 1944, and grew up in an industrial part of Yorkshire. His parents were both teachers, but a family friend he admired was in the British navy, and as a boy, Ian wanted to follow in that man's footsteps. This dream ended when Wilmut found out during his teen years that the navy would never accept him because he was color-blind.

Wilmut's next love was farming, because he enjoyed being outdoors and knew that a farmer's life would keep him outside much of the time. Working on farms during weekends, he milked dairy cows and saw them giving birth. Those experiences interested him in the animals' biology.

Wilmut enrolled in the agricultural college of the University of Nottingham with the plan of becoming a dairy farmer, but he soon decided that he would be a failure at the business side of farming. A summer job in 1966, just before the start of his senior year, turned his thinking in a different direction. Wilmut's work in the laboratory of Christopher Polge, a scientist at Cambridge University, introduced him to embryos—living things in an early stage of development, before birth. Animal embryos are just barely visible to the naked eye, but under a microscope, Wilmut told an interviewer for the online educational organization Academy of Achievement in 1998, "they're extremely beautiful little things."

Newly fascinated with the process of development, Wilmut changed his focus of study to embryology, which studies that process. After graduating from Nottingham in 1967 with a bachelor of science degree in agriculture, he returned to Polge's laboratory. Polge was developing ways to freeze sperm from prize pigs, cattle, and other farm animals so that it could be stored for later use

Ian Wilmut's production of a cloned sheep from a mature cell, announced in 1997, triggered fears that humans would soon be cloned. (Roslin Institute)

in artificial insemination. Wilmut earned his Ph.D. from Darwin College, Cambridge, in 1971 by creating a technique for freezing boar (male pig) sperm.

Wilmut also did his postdoctoral work with Polge, helping to produce Frosty, the first calf to be born from an embryo that had been frozen and thawed, in early 1973. In October of that same year, Wilmut moved to what was then called the Animal Breeding Research Station, a government agricultural laboratory located in Roslin, Scotland, a quiet village not far from Edinburgh. This facility was renamed the Roslin Institute in 1993.

A Change of Focus

Wilmut's first project at the research station, which specialized in the genetics of farm animals, was trying to find out why so many embryos die before they finish developing. About a quarter of fertilized eggs from cattle and sheep fail to produce living offspring, for instance. This high rate of loss was expensive for farmers, and Wilmut hoped that learning its causes might reveal ways to reduce it.

In the early 1980s, however, a new director, Roger Land, took over the Roslin laboratory and changed its research focus to the genetic engineering of farm animals. Land told Wilmut to stop his embryo studies and, instead, find ways to put human genes into the fertilized eggs of cattle and sheep, in the hope of creating animals that would produce medically valuable human proteins in their milk. Being forced to abandon the project he had been working on for years made Wilmut so angry that he almost quit, but he finally decided to stay because he and his wife did not want to leave their rural home or make their three children change schools.

Inserting genes into the eggs of mammals, Wilmut (like many other scientists of the time) soon found out, was not as easy as putting DNA into bacteria. Genetically engineered mice, the first genetically altered mammals, had been produced in 1980, but one technique that worked on the mice could not be used on large farm animals because the kind of cell the procedure depended upon had not yet been located in these animals.

CONNECTIONS: PHARMING

Herbert Boyer and other genetic engineering pioneers of the late 1970s made bacteria into "factories" producing insulin and other human proteins that could be sold as drugs. About 10 years later, researchers and businesspeople began developing ways to do the same with cattle, sheep, and other farm animals. The drug substances usually appeared in the animals' milk. In a pun based on the fact that *pharm-*, a word root meaning "drug," is pronounced the same as *farm*, the use of animals to make drugs came to be known as pharming.

Researchers first produced genetically altered, or transgenic, farm animals in 1985. As Ian Wilmut and other scientists learned, however, the process was difficult at best, and no one could guarantee that the offspring of a transgenic and a normal animal would carry the altered genes. Cloning was the only way to produce relatively large numbers of animals carrying the same inserted genes. Drug companies were therefore eager to support Wilmut and other scientists who studied animal cloning.

As of the early 2000s, transgenic "pharm" animals, cloned or otherwise, have been produced only in small numbers. Probably for this reason, they have not caused as much controversy as genetically altered plants, which are much more common. Some environmentalist and animal rights groups, however, say that such animals should not be produced. Animal rights supporters point out that some transgenic animals have suffered severe and painful health problems. Environmentalists worry about a transgenic salmon, developed in 2000, that grows twice as fast as normal salmon. They fear that the genetically modified fish could crowd out wild salmon if it escaped into rivers. The developers of the salmon say that the altered fish will be unable to reproduce, however.

A fertilized egg cell gives rise to all the cells in a living thing's body, so this single cell has the power to become skin, bone, muscle, or any other type of cell. Most cells lose that flexibility as the unborn organism begins to develop, but a few cells in early embryos, called embryonic stem cells, retain it. Two scientists in England had extracted embryonic stem cells from mice in 1981 and developed ways to grow the cells in the laboratory. Researchers found that if they modified the genes of embryonic stem cells and implanted the cells in mouse embryos, some of the cells in the resulting mice would contain the altered genes. Wilmut tried to isolate stem cells from sheep and cattle embryos during the mid-1980s, but he never succeeded.

Rumors of Cloning

Implanting altered stem cells in embryos was not the only possible way of creating multiple copies of genetically engineered animals. "It soon occurred to me," Wilmut wrote in *The Second Creation*, a book about the development of Dolly that he coauthored with fellow Roslin researcher Keith Campbell and science writer Colin Tudge, "that it would be better if we could first allow the zygote [fertilized egg] to multiply, to produce several or many cells, then add new DNA to several or many of those cells, and then produce new embryos from each of the transformed cells. Such multiplication is cloning." With cloning, each successful gene transfer could produce many embryos instead of just one.

Robert Briggs and Thomas J. King, developmental biologists at the Institute for Cancer Research (later the Fox Chase Cancer Center) in Philadelphia, had cloned frogs in 1952 through a process called somatic cell nuclear transfer, in which they removed the nucleus from a fertilized frog egg and combined the egg with a cell from a frog embryo in an early stage of development. Substances in the cytoplasm of the egg somehow reprogrammed the genes in the added nucleus so that the combined cell became able to produce a whole frog embryo and, eventually, a tadpole. All the cells in the tadpole contained the same genes as the nucleus donor, which meant that the tadpole was a clone of the frog from which the donor cell came. Davor Solter of the University of Pennsylvania and others adapted this technique for use in mice, but the resulting embryos usually did not develop to produce baby mice. By the mid-1980s, most scientists had concluded that the nuclear transfer—and probably any other cloning technique—would not work with mammals.

Ian Wilmut shared this view until a fellow researcher told him during an after-hours chat at a scientific meeting in early 1986 that

Steen Willadsen, a Danish-born scientist, had cloned calves from single cells taken from embryos in a late stage of development. This claim astounded Wilmut, since all cells in late embryos were thought to have become specialized. Had Willadsen finally found cattle stem cells—or, more thrilling still, had he discovered a way to make nuclear transfer work with specialized cells?

Willadsen had not published an account of his work, so Wilmut tracked him down in Canada, where the Danish researcher was then living, and asked him if the rumor was true. Willadsen said it was. He described his technique, which included using unfertilized rather than fertilized eggs and employing a tiny jolt of electricity to make the nucleus-free egg and the body cell fuse together. Returning to the Roslin institute, Wilmut persuaded Roger Land to let him try to duplicate and extend Willadsen's experiments.

Stopping Cells in Their Tracks

As cells grow and divide, they move through different stages of what is called the cell cycle. During one stage, for instance, they duplicate their DNA, and during the next stage they check the copies for mistakes. Around 1990, Lawrence Smith, a graduate student in Wilmut's laboratory, discovered that nuclear transfer was more likely to succeed during some parts of the cell cycle than others. Having both the egg and the cell donating the nucleus in the same phase of the cycle also seemed to be important.

Wilmut hired Keith Campbell, an English cell biologist, in 1991 to help him investigate Smith's findings. Campbell decided that in order to find out which part of the cell cycle worked best for cloning, he needed to have large numbers of cells in the same phase of the cycle at the same time. One possible way to put cells in step with each other, he thought, might be to starve them. He knew that when a cell is deprived of nutrients, it protects itself by stopping its division and going into a quiet state until food becomes available again. (This resting stage is a normal part of the cell cycle, but it lasts longer than usual if a cell lacks nutrients.) If Campbell limited nutrients in dishes full of cells, he guessed, then all the cells in the dishes would enter the resting state.

Campbell's plan succeeded. The starvation procedure not only put large groups of cells in the same stage of the cell cycle but, when the cells were used as donors in nuclear transfer, seemed to make the genes in the transferred nuclei more able to respond to the cytoplasm's reprogramming than they had been before. As a result, more of the combined cells produced embryos. Furthermore, cloning done with starved cells worked equally well regardless of the age of the embryo from which the cells came or the length of time the cells had been grown in the laboratory. In other words, as Willadsen's work had suggested, specialized as well as unspecialized cells could be cloned.

Taking Cloning All the Way

Wilmut and Campbell used their revised nuclear transfer technique on unfertilized sheep eggs, which they combined with cells from sheep embryos in a late stage of development. Most of the embryos made from the combined cells died, as the researchers had expected, but a few survived. When these grew large enough, Wilmut and Campbell transplanted them into sheep surrogate mothers. Finally, in July 1995, the Roslin team produced their first cloned animals, two Welsh Mountain ewes (female sheep) that they named Megan and Morag.

Wilmut and Campbell wondered how far they could take their success. Almost as a joke, they decided to see whether they could reprogram a mature cell from an adult animal to make it able to manufacture an entire embryo. PPL Therapeutics, a company founded in 1987 to commercialize Roslin's products, agreed to fund the experiment, hoping that the cloning technique could be used to create duplicates of animals genetically engineered to produce proteins useful in medicine.

The Birth of Dolly

Wilmut and Campbell decided to work with a dish of cells that they found in a PPL freezer, which happened to be mammary (breast) cells from a six-year-old Finn Dorset ewe. They performed the nuclear

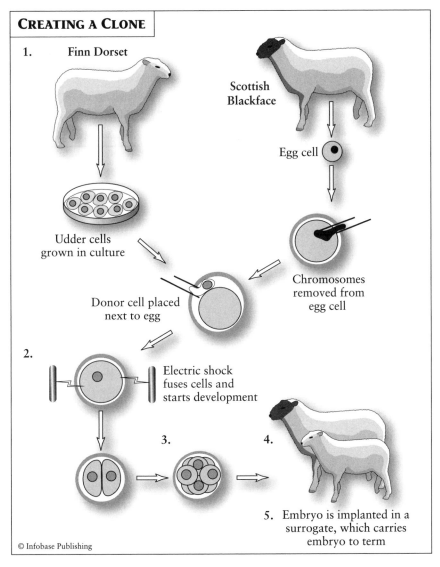

CREATING A CLONE

1. Finn Dorset

Scottish Blackface

Egg cell

Udder cells grown in culture

Chromosomes removed from egg cell

Donor cell placed next to egg

2. Electric shock fuses cells and starts development

3.

4.

5. Embryo is implanted in a surrogate, which carries embryo to term

© Infobase Publishing

In the procedure used to produce Dolly, the cloned sheep, Ian Wilmut's team took unfertilized egg cells from a normal female sheep and removed the DNA-containing nucleus from them (step 1). The researchers used a tiny electric current to make these eggs combine, or fuse, with mature cells from the udder of another adult sheep, which had been grown in culture dishes and starved to put them in a resting state (step 2). The combined cells were allowed to grow in culture until they reached an early stage of embryonic development, called a blastocyst (step 3). Each microscopic embryo was then transferred to the uterus of a surrogate mother (step 4). Out of 277 tries, only Dolly developed fully and survived long enough to be born (step 5).

transfer procedure on these mature cells and also, for comparison purposes, on cells from sheep embryos and fetuses of different ages (fetuses are unborn living things at a later stage of development than embryos). The team eventually obtained seven lambs from the fetal and embryo cells, but only one lamb that came from an adult cell survived until birth. This remarkable animal was finally born on July 5, 1996. The Roslin group named her Dolly, after singer-actress Dolly Parton.

Dolly's first few months of life were as quiet as her birth. Wilmut's team watched the lamb carefully to make sure that she remained healthy, and they carried out tests to confirm that she was genetically identical to the ewe cell that had given rise to her. They did not tell newspapers about their achievement because the respected science magazine *Nature,* which had accepted their scientific paper about Dolly, had a rule that research described in its pages could not be publicly announced before an article's publication date. PPL Therapeutics also wanted the story kept quiet until it obtained a patent on the technology that Wilmut and Campbell had used.

A Media Uproar

The silence surrounding Dolly ended abruptly. The *Observer,* a London newspaper, broke the story on February 22, 1997, almost a week ahead of *Nature*'s schedule. The *New York Times* followed with its own front-page article the next day. Other media quickly picked up the news, and the tale of Dolly's birth—and what it might mean in terms of human cloning—spread around the world.

Wilmut and the Roslin team had expected some media attention, but they were astounded by the furor that occurred. "Nothing could have prepared us for the thousands of telephone calls (literally), the scores of interviews, the offers of tours and contracts, and in some cases the opprobrium [strong disapproval], though much less of that than we might have feared," Wilmut wrote in *The Second Creation.*

As the leader of the research group, Wilmut had to answer most of the reporters' questions. The most common question was whether the Roslin scientists planned to create a cloned human baby. Over and over, Wilmut said he had no such intention and, indeed, saw

PARALLELS: TEST-TUBE BABIES

An earlier method of altering human reproduction created an uproar much like the one that followed the birth of Dolly. In the early 1970s, two British scientists, embryologist Robert Edwards and surgeon Patrick Steptoe, developed a method of removing eggs from a woman's ovaries and fertilizing them in the laboratory, usually with sperm from the woman's husband. Once an embryo started to grow, it was implanted in the mother's (or sometimes a surrogate mother's) uterus to continue developing into a baby. This technique, called in vitro ("in glass") fertilization, was designed to help couples who could not have children in the common way because, for instance, the tubes that carry eggs from the woman's ovaries to her uterus were blocked or damaged.

Louise Brown, the first baby to be produced by in vitro fertilization, was born on July 25, 1978. Like Dolly, she was the only success among many failures (102, in the human case). Just as happened with cloning after Dolly's birth, some scientists said the procedure was too unsafe to use in humans, and some religious leaders claimed that creation of so-called test-tube babies ("petri-dish babies" would be a more accurate term) like Brown was immoral because it separated sex from reproduction.

In vitro fertilization became more reliable as time went on, and as it did so, controversy about it died down. Almost a million children conceived through in vitro fertilization were born in North America and Europe during the 20 years following the procedure's development, and the technique is even more widely used today.

little reason why anyone should do such a risky thing. He pointed out that Dolly was the only successful birth among 277 attempts—hardly encouraging odds for a potential experiment on humans.

Dolly the Star

In the years following Dolly's birth, researchers in many parts of the world cloned different kinds of animals, including mice and even

Dolly appeared to enjoy posing for photographers, as she is doing here with Ian Wilmut. (Roslin Institute)

monkeys, by nuclear transfer. Some of these clones lived normal lives, but others died soon after birth or developed severe health problems that may have been due to their origin.

Dolly herself, meanwhile, seemed to enjoy her life as a media star. Most sheep are shy, backing away when humans come close, but Dolly ran forward to greet visitors. She put her front feet up on the fence around her pen, posed for pictures, and happily accepted petting and treats. Indeed, she was fed so often that she became quite fat. Her extra weight may have been one of the reasons why she developed arthritis at an unusually early age for a sheep. Overall, however, her health remained good. She gave birth, by normal reproductive means, to six healthy lambs.

Unfortunately, when Dolly was about seven and a half years old—late middle age, by sheep standards—she caught a common virus that causes an incurable lung disease. On February 13, 2003, the world's most famous sheep had to be put to sleep.

From Sheep to People

The goal of Ian Wilmut's experiments had been to find a way to clone genetically altered farm animals, and he eventually succeeded. In July 1997, the Roslin team announced the birth of another lamb, Polly, that was both a clone (from the cell of a fetus) and genetically engineered. The cell that gave rise to Polly had been given a human gene that made her milk contain clotting factor 9, one of several proteins that people with the inherited blood disease hemophilia must take.

Wilmut and other researchers at Roslin and elsewhere have also explored the possibility of adding human genes to pigs so that pig

SOCIAL IMPACT: HUMAN CLONING

Concern about possible use of cloning to create human children reached fever pitch in the years following Dolly's birth, particularly after several groups, ranging from the Italian fertility specialist Severino Antinori to a flying saucer cult called the Raelians, announced (without supporting evidence) that they were about to produce or had produced a cloned child. The Council of Europe banned this kind of cloning, called reproductive cloning, on January 12, 1998, and at least two dozen individual nations have also banned or placed a moratorium on the activity. The United States has not yet passed a law banning reproductive cloning, but several states have done so, and most Americans seem to feel that it should be forbidden.

Objections to creating a cloned child reach far beyond the practical issue of safety. Some critics say that cloning humans would be "playing God." Others fear that the parents of cloned children, or the children themselves, would see the children as mere products rather than independent human beings. Producers of clones might expect to see exact duplicates of themselves, lost loved ones, or famous people chosen as the source of the clones.

Defenders of cloning say that clones would simply be delayed twins, no less human than natural identical twins.

organs might be transplanted into people, easing the great shortage of available organs that exists today. Pigs and humans are genetically similar in many ways, but they are different enough that the human immune system normally destroys pig tissue placed in the body. The scientists hope that added genes will make proteins that fool the immune system into accepting the pig organs as human.

In the early 2000s, Ian Wilmut changed the direction of his research from animals to humans. Although he still despises the idea of creating cloned babies, he does want to clone human embryos to make supplies of embryonic stem cells and other cells for use in research. Such embryos are allowed to develop only to the size of a few hundred cells.

British law allows this kind of human cloning, which is called research cloning or therapeutic cloning. Any researcher who plans to carry out therapeutic cloning, however, must obtain a permit from a government agency called the Human Fertilization and Embryology Authority. On October 26, 2004, once again leading his field, Ian Wilmut requested such a permit. The authority granted Wilmut the permit on February 8, 2005. The agency had given a similar license to only one other research group.

Wilmut told the agency that he wants to clone embryos from cells of people with amyotrophic lateral sclerosis (ALS, or Lou Gehrig's disease, one of a group of illnesses called motor neurone disease in Britain), an incurable nerve disease that causes slow paralysis and eventual death. Wilmut plans to take stem cells from the embryos and make them develop into nerve cells. He hopes to learn how developing nerve cells from people with ALS differ from nerve cells made by normal embryos. That information might shed light on the cause of this disease, which is presently unknown, or perhaps even lead to a treatment for it.

Wilmut has received many awards for his work, including the Order of the British Empire (1999). Other prizes he has won include the Lord Lloyd of Kilgerran Prize and the Research Medal of the Royal Agricultural Society of England. In 2002, Germany's Ernst Schering Foundation awarded him the Ernst Schering Prize. He won the Paul Ehrlich and Ludwig Darmstaedter Prize from Frankfurt (Germany) University in 2005.

In addition to continuing his research at Roslin, Ian Wilmut travels around the world to speak about cloning and other ethical issues in biotechnology. He has written numerous popular as well as scientific articles and has coauthored a book about the creation of Dolly and her importance. Wilmut remains a leader in both the scientific development of cloning and discussions about what cloning might mean for the world.

Chronology

1944	Ian Wilmut born in Hampton Lucy, England, on July 7
1952	Robert Briggs and Thomas J. King clone frogs by somatic cell nuclear transfer
1971	Wilmut earns Ph.D. from Cambridge University by developing a way to freeze boar sperm
1973	Wilmut produces Frosty, the first calf grown from an embryo that had been frozen and thawed
	Wilmut takes job with Animal Breeding Research Station in Roslin, Scotland, and begins project to learn why so many embryos die before completing development
1980	First genetically altered mammals (mice) produced
1981	British scientists extract embryonic stem cells from mice and grow the cells in laboratory dishes
1980s	Early in the decade, Wilmut is forced to change research focus to genetic engineering of farm animals
	Wilmut unsuccessfully seeks embryonic stem cells in sheep and cattle in mid-decade
1985	First genetically altered farm animals produced
1986	Wilmut learns that Steen Willadsen has cloned calves from cells of late embryos and decides to duplicate and extend this work
1990	Lawrence Smith finds that nuclear transfer works better in some stages of the cell cycle than others and that having both egg and nucleus donor in the same stage of the cycle also helps the process succeed

1990s	Early in the decade, cell biologist Keith Campbell finds that starving cells not only puts all the cells in the same stage of the cell cycle but improves the effectiveness of nuclear transfer
1991	Campbell joins Wilmut's group
1993	Animal Breeding Research Station becomes Roslin Institute
1995	Megan and Morag, first sheep cloned from cultured (late embryo) cells, born in July
1996	Dolly born on July 5
1997	On February 22, London *Observer* publishes story announcing Dolly's birth Roslin team announces the birth of Polly, a sheep that is both cloned and genetically altered, in July
1998	On January 12, Council of Europe bans reproductive cloning in European Union
1999	Wilmut made an officer of the Order of the British Empire in June
2000s	Early in the decade, researchers clone many kinds of mammals Early in the decade, several groups announce plans to clone a human baby, but none proves that it has done so
2003	On February 13, Dolly is put to sleep after developing an incurable lung infection
2005	On February 8, Britain's Human Fertilization and Embryology Authority grants Ian Wilmut permission to clone human embryos for research purposes

Further Reading

Books

Kolata, Gina. *Clone: The Road to Dolly, and the Path Ahead.* New York: William Morrow, 1999.
    Describes the experiments that led to Dolly's creation but focuses on the potential ethical significance of human cloning.

Wilmut, Ian, Keith Campbell, and Colin Tudge. *The Second Creation: Dolly and the Age of Biological Control.* New York: Farrar, Straus & Giroux, 2000.
> Provides scientific background for the story of Dolly's development. Somewhat difficult reading.

Articles

"Ian Wilmut, Ph.D." Academy of Achievement, Hall of Science and Exploration. Available online. URL: www.achievement.org/autodoc/page/wil0int-1. Posted on May 23, 1998. Accessed on September 15, 2004.
> Lengthy interview with Wilmut, in six parts, discusses his background and career, the development of Dolly, and Wilmut's opinions on the implications of cloning.

Ibrahim, Youssef M. "Ian Wilmut: For Scientist, Secrecy Gives Way to Spotlight," *New York Times,* 24 February 1997, pp. C17, B8.
> Extensive biographical article about Wilmut, published shortly after Dolly's birth was announced.

Kolata, Gina. "Scientist Reports First Cloning Ever of Adult Mammal," *New York Times,* 23 February 1997, p. 1.
> First newspaper story in the United States to describe the birth of Dolly.

"Wilmut, Ian." *Current Biography Yearbook 1997,* 624–626. New York: H. W. Wilson, 1997.
> Detailed biographical profile of Wilmut, including quotes from multiple interviews.

Wilmut, I., and others. "Viable Offspring Derived from Fetal and Adult Mammalian Cells," *Nature,* 27 February 1997, pp. 810–813.
> Scientific article that describes how Dolly was created.

8

OUT OF ONE, MANY

JAMES THOMSON AND EMBRYONIC STEM CELLS

Some animals have an ability that seems almost magic. If a cat grabs a lizard's tail, the lizard can drop the tail from its body and then grow another. A frog can replace a lost leg. If a worm is cut in half, each half can regenerate into a whole new worm. Humans, however, cannot regrow lost body parts.

Or can they? Some researchers think that in the future, people may be able to regenerate tissues and perhaps even organs lost to injury or disease. The key to this achievement lies in cells that, like the legendary Peter Pan, never grow up. James Thomson, a scientist at the University of Wisconsin in Madison, discovered these startling cells.

Versatile Cells

Until work and family took up all his time, James Alexander Thomson loved flying or hang gliding over the Wisconsin hills. His research has also sent him on some risky flights.

Thomson was born on December 20, 1958, in Chicago and grew up in Oak Park, a Chicago suburb. His father was an accountant, his mother a secretary. Inspired partly by an uncle who was a rocket scientist at the National Aeronautics and Space Administration (NASA), Thomson decided at an early age that he wanted to enter science. He studied biophysics at the Urbana-Champaign campus of the University of Illinois, graduating with a B.S. in 1981. His outstanding grades earned him membership in the honor society Phi Beta Kappa.

Thomson became interested in the way living things develop before birth while still an undergraduate. He learned that a human body contains 220 different kinds of cells—nerve cells, muscle cells, skin cells, and many more. Each type of cells has its own shape, activities, and set of proteins. Once a cell takes on the characteristics of a particular cell type, it is said to be differentiated. At the time, most scientists believed that fully differentiated cells could not produce cells of types other than their own, even though all cells in a living thing's body contain the same genes and are the descendants of a single cell, the fertilized egg.

Only the fertilized egg has the power to make all the cell types in a living body, as well as the cells that will nourish the growing embryo. Researchers began to suspect in the early 1950s, however,

James Thomson's discovery of human embryonic stem cells may lead to revolutionary medical treatments, but research on these cells has also caused controversy because embryos must be destroyed in order to harvest them. (Jeff Miller/University of Wisconsin, Madison)

I WAS THERE: SHEETS OF SKIN

During the late 1970s, Howard Green and James Rheinwald developed a technique for multiplying adult skin stem cells into a sheet of outer skin, or epidermis, in the laboratory. The sheet, as fragile as tissue paper, could be attached to a thin layer of gauze and placed over a burn or other wound. After a week, the new skin blended into the healthy skin around the wound, and the gauze could be removed.

People with severe burns are usually treated by cutting skin from unburned parts of their bodies and transplanting, or grafting, the skin onto the burned areas. In a few cases, however, so much of a person's body is burned that there is not enough healthy skin left to graft. In *The Proteus Effect,* a book about stem cell research, Ann B. Parson describes a disaster of this kind that occurred in Cambridge, Massachusetts, in 1983. Two brothers, five and six years old, suffered burns on more than 95 percent of their bodies when one of them struck a match as they were cleaning themselves with a solvent after a painting project. The solvent ignited explosively, burning the boys and a third child, who died.

John Remensnyder, a surgeon at the Shriners Burn Institute, asked Green, then at Harvard Medical School, for help in saving the lives of the surviving boys by expanding the tiny patches of skin that could be taken from them into sheets large enough to cover their wounds. By

---

that embryos might contain some cells that were almost as versatile. These cells, as yet undiscovered, were given the name *stem cells* because cells of more specific types stem, or descend, from them. Some scientists also predicted that tissues replaced often in adult animals, such as skin and blood, would prove to contain stem cells.

In 1960, Ernest McCulloch and James Till of the Ontario Cancer Center in Canada identified the first known type of adult stem cells in mice. These cells, located in the bone marrow (the fatty material inside some bones), make all the types of cells in the blood. Howard Green and James Rheinwald, working at the Massachusetts Institute of Technology, succeeded in growing human adult skin stem cells from a newborn child in 1974 (stem cells from any stage of development later

then, Green had tested his cultured skin on human patients, but only on small burns. He had never grown skin on anything like the scale that would be needed here. Nonetheless, he and everyone else in his laboratory agreed to try. Parson reports:

> Green, his five postdoctoral fellows, and two technicians rolled into action. . . . They would culture 146 grafts from one brother, and as many as 233 grafts for the other brother. . . . Each graft measured approximately seven square inches. When early-morning surgery was called for, Green and his team would arrive in the lab by 5 A.M. in order to give themselves time to staple the specimens into a gauze backing for easier handling, set them back into petri dishes, package the dishes in boxes, gas and seal the boxes to ensure germ-free air quality, and oversee the boxes' transport to Shriners. . . .
>
> [During the next few weeks] the Shriners staff would witness what amounted to a miracle. Small patches of skin salvaged from the armpits of each boy and expanded 10,000-fold in Green's lab meant the difference between life and death for each brother. In essence, the stem cells in those remaining underarm patches of epidermis saved their lives. . . . "It was the first demonstration that human stem cells of any type could be expanded substantially in culture and used to permanently restore a patient's lost tissue," says Rheinwald.

than that of the embryo are considered "adult"). No one, however, could find embryonic stem cells.

Hunting an Elusive Quarry

James Thomson, or Jamie, as his friends called him, learned about stem cells when he continued his embryology studies at the University of Pennsylvania in the early 1980s. There he worked under Davor Solter, who was studying a strange kind of cancer in mice. This cancer, called a teratoma or teratocarcinoma, is essentially an embryo whose development has become completely disorganized. A teratoma contains many kinds of differentiated cells—muscle, skin, even sometimes hair and teeth—but instead of forming the complex structures that make up a living thing, the cells mix together in a chaotic jumble. Researchers in the 1960s had shown that all the differentiated cells in a teratoma came from a single cell.

At the time, most of what scientists knew or guessed about embryonic stem cells came from research on mouse teratomas, because researchers had not been able to isolate stem cells from normal embryos. Only in 1981, the year Thomson began his graduate training, did two scientists at Cambridge University in England, Matthew Kaufman and Martin Evans, report that they had found such cells in normal mouse embryos and persuaded the cells to multiply dependably in laboratory culture dishes. The cells came from embryos at the stage of development called the blastocyst, when the tiny embryo, ready to be implanted in the mother's uterus, consists of a hollow ball of cells. The stem cells bulged from the inner wall of the blastocyst.

Thomson earned a degree in veterinary medicine from the University of Pennsylvania in 1985 and a Ph.D. in molecular biology from the same university in 1988. Shortly afterward, he spent a few months in the laboratory of embryologist Colin Stewart at the Roche Institute of Molecular Biology in New Jersey, learning how to extract embryonic stem cells from mice. Thomson mentioned to Stewart that he was going to do postdoctoral research on primate embryology at the Oregon Regional Primate Center in Beaverton, and the two discussed the possibility of extracting and growing embryonic stem cells from monkeys or other nonhuman primates. If that could be done, Stewart said, it might pave the way for isolating human embryonic stem cells as well. "It was the first time I had thought about human [embryonic stem] cells at all," Thomson said later.

From Mice to Monkeys

After completing his postdoctoral stint at Beaverton, Thomson moved to the Wisconsin Regional Primate Research Center, part of the University of Wisconsin at Madison, in June 1991 and joined a project to isolate embryonic stem cells from primates that had recently been established there. Thomson found that removing early embryos from female monkeys and extracting stem cells from the tiny blastocysts were challenging tasks, but making the stem cells grow and divide in laboratory dishes without differentiating into specific cell types (bone, muscle, nerve, and so on), as they would have done in a normal embryo, was harder still. Thomson modified the technique that Evans and Kaufman had used with their mouse embryo cells, placing the monkey cells on top of a layer of a certain type of mouse cell that survived well in culture. This bottom sheet of cells, termed "feeder" cells, produced growth factors and other substances that nourished the embryo cells.

In August 1995, Thomson published a report saying that he had isolated stem cells from rhesus macaque monkey embryos and made the cells grow in his laboratory for almost two years without differentiating. This was the first time that embryonic stem cells from primates had been separated from embryos and grown in this way.

Controversial Research

Thomson's breakthrough attracted more than scientific attention. Just days after his monkey report appeared, Michael West, an entrepreneur who headed a California biotechnology company called Geron Corporation, paid the Wisconsin scientist a visit. The name of West's company, which came from a Greek word meaning "old man," reflected West's interest in finding a way to halt human aging. West believed that human embryonic stem cells, if they could be isolated, might be harnessed to achieve his aim. If Thomson would try to find these cells, West said, Geron would pay for most of the research.

Finding funding was important, because Thomson could not ask the National Institutes of Health or any other federal agency for a grant, as many other scientists did. Laws passed in the late 1980s and early 1990s stated that federal funds could not be used for research on tissue from human fetuses (unborn humans after more than seven weeks of development), and, although the laws were not entirely clear, they seemed likely to apply to research on embryos as well. Thomson therefore would need private funding if he wished to seek human embryonic stem cells.

The restrictive laws had been passed because many people saw research on embryos and fetuses as unethical—perhaps even a kind of murder. These people believed that an unborn child was a separate individual, entitled to full human rights, from the time the fertilized egg was formed. It therefore should not be experimented upon or killed, as would be necessary to harvest stem cells. Even some scientists thought that research should be confined to adult stem cells, which had been found in many tissues. Adult stem cells in animals, however, could not produce as wide a variety of differentiated cells as embryonic stem cells could. For this reason, other researchers, including Thomson, believed that human embryonic stem cells would provide more effective medical treatments than adult stem cells would.

James Thomson thought long and hard about the ethical issues involved before deciding whether to extend his research to humans. He also discussed his project with R. Alta Charo and Norman Fost, bioethicists employed by the university. Fost told Ann Parson, "Jamie [Thomson] cared deeply about doing the right thing. He appreciated the larger social context and understood that others might be upset about what he was doing."

The embryos Thomson planned to use would come from the university's fertility clinic. During artificial insemination, fertility clinics normally fertilize about a dozen eggs at a time. The two or three healthiest of the resulting embryos are implanted in the mother's uterus (several embryos are implanted to increase the chances that at least one will complete the development process and produce a baby). The rest of the embryos are frozen and stored for possible later use. A 2003 estimate stated that about 400,000 frozen embryos were stored in the United States alone. If not implanted in mothers, these embryos are eventually discarded or, if the parents give their permission, used for research.

Thomson and the university ethicists eventually decided that Thomson's project would be ethical. First, it potentially could help people suffering from incurable diseases because stem cells might be used to grow tissues for transplantation. Second, the work would use only embryos that would be destroyed anyway. "I could not

see that throwing them [the embryos] out was better" than using
them for lifesaving research, Thomson told *Time* magazine reporter
Frederic Golden in 2001. By the end of 1995, the university's insti-
tutional review board had given Thomson permission to go ahead
with his project, and the Wisconsin Alumni Research Foundation
(WARF) had agreed to provide the rest of the funding he needed.

A Groundbreaking Announcement

Thomson expected that, just as in mice and monkeys, embryonic
stem cells in human embryos would grow from the inner wall of the
blastocyst. The fertility clinic embryos, however, presented a problem that had not arisen in the animal experiments. Fertility clinics
froze embryos the day after fertilization, and as far as Thomson
knew, thawed embryos had been made to develop in a laboratory
for only about two more days before dying. Human embryos do not
form blastocysts until about five days after fertilization.

Unable to produce human blastocysts, Thomson was stymied
until May 1996, when he learned that David Gardner, an Australian
scientist, had invented a way to keep human embryos growing in
laboratory dishes long enough to reach this stage of development.
After much struggle, Jeff Jones, an embryologist in the university's
in vitro fertilization laboratory, succeeded in adapting Gardner's
technique to Thomson's needs. Thomson's laboratory grew their
first human blastocysts with this procedure in January 1998.

Thomson extracted stem cells from his blastocysts and then began
culturing them, at first using the same procedures he had applied to
monkey stem cells. As with the monkey cells, the most difficult part
of the task was persuading the cells to continue dividing in dishes
indefinitely, without differentiating. The best way to do this proved
to be to keep the stem cell population in each culture dish low, moving some cells to a new dish whenever an existing dish began to be
crowded. Thomson had to get up early every morning for six months
to check on his cells and replate them if necessary.

On November 6, 1998, Thomson and his coworkers published a
paper in the respected American journal *Science,* stating that their
laboratory had kept human embryonic stem cells reproducing in cul-

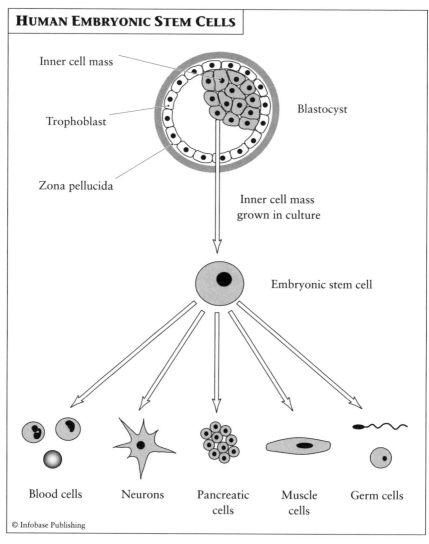

HUMAN EMBRYONIC STEM CELLS

Inner cell mass

Trophoblast

Blastocyst

Zona pellucida

Inner cell mass
grown in culture

Embryonic stem cell

Blood cells   Neurons   Pancreatic   Muscle   Germ cells
cells   cells

© Infobase Publishing

To produce human embryonic stem cells, James Thomson used embryos that had been created in fertility clinics by in vitro fertilization and then frozen. Such embryos are eventually discarded if the parents do not use them. Thomson allowed the embryos to develop in culture until they formed a hollow ball called a blastocyst. He took stem cells from the inner wall of the blastocyst and allowed them to grow further in culture. The cells can be kept in an undifferentiated (immature) state, or they can be allowed to form different kinds of mature cells, such as blood cells, nerve cells, or muscle cells.

ture without differentiating for five months and had established five independent cell lines. All the cells in each cell line were descended from a single founder cell and therefore contained exactly the same genes. Four days later, John Gearhart of Johns Hopkins University in Baltimore announced that he had grown embryonic stem cells derived from primordial germ cells (the precursors of sperm and eggs) taken from human fetuses aborted for medical reasons.

Media Storm

Thomson's announcement, coming only about a year and a half after Ian Wilmut's revelation that he had cloned a sheep, aroused a predict-

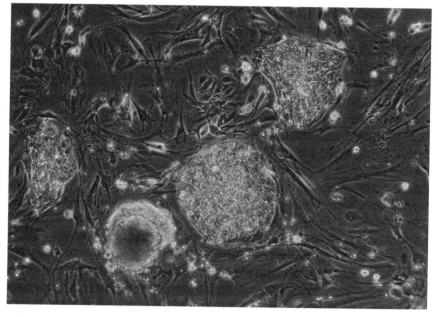

This microphotograph shows human embryonic stem cells growing in culture, enlarged 10 times. The rounded, dense masses of cells are stem cell colonies. The long cells between the masses are a type of mouse cells used as a "feeder layer" to produce nutrients that help the stem cells survive and grow. (University of Wisconsin, Madison)

able storm of controversy. Many scientists, including Harold Varmus, then the director of the National Institutes of Health, and Tommy Thompson, the governor of Wisconsin and President George W. Bush's choice for the post of secretary of health and human services, praised Thomson's work. "This research has the potential to revolutionize the practice of medicine and improve the quality and length of life," Varmus told a U.S. Senate hearing less than a month after Thomson's publication, according to an article by Terry Devitt on the University of Wisconsin stem cell Web site. "Right-to-life" groups, however, said that research on human embryonic stem cells should be outlawed because embryos had to be killed in order to remove stem cells from them.

Although he was not surprised by the ethical firestorm, Thomson, whom a university acquaintance (according to Ann Parson) calls "relentlessly quiet," found it as distracting and annoying as Ian Wilmut had found the furor after the announcement of Dolly's birth. Thomson later complained to Terry Devitt that as far as his own research was concerned, "the first year or two [after isolation of human embryonic stem cells] were pretty much wasted due to politics."

Some statements from Thomson's supporters disturbed him almost as much as those from critics. Certain boosters of embryonic stem cell research implied that cures for illnesses such as diabetes and Alzheimer's disease would be available within a few years if the research was allowed to proceed without restrictions. Thomson, by contrast, realized that doctors would not be able to use such treatments for at least a decade—if ever. Many improvements would have to be made before the stem cells could be grown in large quantities, and many tests would have to take place to find out whether the cells could actually replace those destroyed by disease.

Presidential Compromise

Soon after President George W. Bush took office in 2001, he addressed the issue of whether stem cell research using human embryos should be eligible for federal funding. Trying to steer a path between those who praised embryonic stem cells' medical promise

ISSUES: EMBRYOS MADE TO ORDER

As the 21st century begins, the debate about embryonic stem cell research has joined the arguments about human cloning because some scientists, including Ian Wilmut, the creator of the cloned sheep Dolly, want to use cloning to make human embryos for the sole purpose of harvesting their stem cells. Wilmut hopes to make embryos from cells of people with certain diseases and study the resulting embryonic stem cells as a way of learning about the diseases. Eventually, other researchers propose, healthy cells from a sick person's body could be cloned into an embryo that would yield stem cells, and the stem cells in turn could be used to grow tissues or organs that would be transplanted into the person. Because the transplants would carry the individual's own genes, the immune system would not destroy them, as happens with transplants from other people unless the transplant recipient takes drugs to suppress the system.

Almost everyone seems to object to reproductive human cloning, or cloning to create a baby, but polls show much more divided feelings about therapeutic cloning, or cloning to create embryos for research or medical treatment. Some people support therapeutic cloning because of its potential power to save lives, while others find the idea of creating embryos in order to destroy them even more repulsive than destroying existing embryos. So far the issue is only theoretical because no one has made a cloned human embryo develop in the laboratory as far as the blastocyst stage, when stem cells can be harvested.

and those who saw destroying embryos as murder, Bush announced on August 9, 2001, that research on the 64 embryonic cell lines already in existence could receive federal money, but government funds could not be used to establish new cell lines, which would require tearing apart additional embryos. As with the earlier ban, scientists could establish new cell lines or carry out other embryo research with private funding, as long as they used only embryos that fertility clincs had planned to discard.

At the time, Thomson and most other scientists welcomed Bush's decision because it allowed at least some embryonic stem cell research to proceed. Carl Gulbrandsen, managing director of the Wisconsin Alumni Research Foundation, told Terry Devitt that "a lot of people

---

SOLVING PROBLEMS: BANKING CORD BLOOD

Embryonic stem cells are not yet usable in medical treatments, but some forms of adult stem cells are. For instance, several kinds of life-threatening blood diseases caused by defects in stem cells in the bone marrow, which form all the cells in the blood, are treated by marrow transplants. Doctors kill the sick people's abnormal marrow cells with drugs or radiation, and then inject healthy marrow cells from a donor. If all goes well, stem cells in the transplanted marrow will rebuild the sick person's blood and immune system. Marrow transplants succeed, however, only if they come from a close relative or an unrelated donor who happens to be very similar genetically to the person receiving the transplant. Otherwise, immune system cells in the donor marrow attack the recipient's body.

A transplant taken from a stored supply of a person's own healthy stem cells would be even more likely to succeed than a marrow transplant from a relative. For this reason, some parents save their newborn baby's umbilical cord, the rope of blood vessels that connects the unborn child to its mother's uterus. The cord, which comes out of the mother along with the baby, can be frozen and stored by companies that specialize in this activity. The umbilical cord contains adult blood-forming stem cells, and if the child ever needs a marrow transplant, blood from the cord can be used instead.

The cord blood might also be able to save another person's life. Studies have shown that cord blood transplants from unrelated donors are less likely to produce immune reactions than marrow transplants. By 2004, several thousand people had received transplants of their own cord blood or that of others. Legislation has been introduced into Congress to establish a network that would collect, maintain, and distribute cord blood for transplants, as the United Network for Organ Sharing currently does with hearts, livers, and other organs.

don't like [Bush's ruling], but it was an ingenious political solution." More recently, however, scientists who depend on federal funding have protested against being restricted to older cell lines because new lines have been established that are likely to be safer and more effective in treating human disease than the first ones.

Making New Cell Types

James Thomson continues to study human embryonic stem cells. He and Dan Kaufman announced in late 2001 that they had made these cells produce many kinds of blood cells by growing the stem cells with blood-forming cells from a mouse. Later, other University of Wisconsin researchers made precursors of nerve cells and heart muscle cells from human embryonic stem cells. Thomson's scientific group has also learned how to change genes in embryonic stem cells so that the cells can be used as laboratory models of human diseases. In 2004, Thomson was focusing his research on finding out how human and nonhuman primate embryonic stem cells "decide" whether to produce more stem cells, make differentiated cells, or die.

In the near term, Thomson has told reporters, he hopes to see human embryonic stem cells used to test drugs and to reveal details about the way normal development takes place. His long-term goals are to find efficient ways to grow these cells in large-scale cultures, to make the cells produce specific types of descendants that will help in medical research, and to work out ways of using transplanted embryonic stem cells as treatments for human diseases.

Thomson is presently the John D. McArthur Professor of Anatomy at the University of Wisconsin at Madison's medical school, as well as chief pathologist at the primate center and the scientific director of the WiCell Research Institute, a nonprofit organization that WARF established in 1999 to support embryonic stem cell research at the university, distribute embryonic cells to other laboratories, and train researchers to work with the cells. Thomson has received several awards, including the Golden Plate Award from the American Academy of Achievement (1999), the Lois Pope LIFE International

Research Award (2002), and the Frank Annunzio Award from the Christopher Columbus Fellowship Foundation (2003). R. Timothy Mulcahy, the associate vice chancellor for research policy at the University of Wisconsin at Madison, told Terry Devitt in 2003, "Thomson's discovery elevated the [stem cell] field to heights previously thought impossible, and has brought within reach all the promise others in the field have long dreamed of."

Chronology

1950s	Early in the decade, researchers begin to suspect that early embryos and some adult tissues contain stem cells, which can produce many different types of cells
1958	James Thomson born in Chicago on December 20
1960	Ernest McCulloch and James Till identify blood-forming stem cells in adult mice
1974	Howard Green and James Rheinwald grow adult skin stem cells from a newborn child
1981	Martin Evans and Matthew Kaufman isolate stem cells from mouse embryos and make them multiply in laboratory dishes
1988	Thomson earns Ph.D. from University of Pennsylvania
1991	In June, Thomson joins Wisconsin Regional Primate Research Center project to find stem cells in monkey embryos
1995	Thomson announces in August that he has isolated embryonic stem cells from monkeys and made the cells grow in culture for two years without differentiating
	A few days later, Michael West of Geron Corporation visits Thomson and offers to fund research aimed at isolating human embryonic stem cells
	Late in the year, after considering ethical issues and obtaining additional funding and permission from the University of Wisconsin, Thomson begins search for human embryonic stem cells

1996	In May, Thomson learns of a procedure for keeping human embryos alive in the laboratory long enough for the embryos to form blastocysts
1998	In January, the Thomson laboratory produces the first blastocysts from fertility clinic embryos
	Thomson publishes an article in the November 6 issue of *Science,* stating that his laboratory has grown human embryonic stem cells in culture for five months without allowing the cells to differentiate
2001	On August 9, President George W. Bush rules that research on existing human embryonic stem cell lines is eligible for federal funding, but research that would create or use new cell lines is not
2003	Thomson receives Frank Annunzio Award from Christopher Columbus Fellowship Foundation

Further Reading

Books

Parson, Ann B. *The Proteus Effect.* Washington, D.C.: Joseph Henry Press, 2004.
> Describes development of stem cell research, including the work of James Thomson.

Articles

Devitt, Terry. "Five Years Later, Stem Cells Still Tantalize." Available online. URL: http://www.news.wisc.edu/packages/stemcells/retro. html. Accessed on December 1, 2004.
> Article describes progress in embryonic stem cell research at the University of Wisconsin, Madison, in the five years after James Thomson first isolated and grew the cells in 1998.

Golden, Frederic. "Stem Winder," *Time,* 20 August 2001, pp. 32–34.
> Interview with Thomson and description of his work, written soon after President Bush's ruling about embryonic stem cell research.

Marshall, Eliot. "A Versatile Cell Line Raises Scientific Hopes, Legal Questions," *Science,* 6 November 1998, p. 1014.
This reporter's article, which appeared in the same issue as Thomson's scientific paper announcing the culturing of human embryonic stem cells, discusses the medical, ethical, and legal implications of Thomson's achievement.
Thomson, James A., et al. "Embryonic Stem Cell Lines Derived from Human Blastocysts," *Science,* 6 November 1998, p. 1,145.
Scientific paper announcing that human embryonic stem cells had been isolated and kept growing in culture for five months without differentiating.
———. "Isolation of Primate Embryonic Stem Cell Line," *Proceedings of the National Academy of Sciences,* 15 August 1995, pp. 7,844–7,848.
Research paper describing the first isolation of embryonic stem cells from primates (rhesus monkeys).
"Thomson, James A." *Current Biography Yearbook 2001,* 550–553. New York: H. W. Wilson Co., 2001.
Biographical profile of Thomson describes his work and contains quotes from interviews.

Web Sites
Embryonic Stem Cells: Research at the University of Wisconsin, Madison. This site, sponsored by the university, provides background and news updates on embryonic stem cell research carried out by James Thomson and others. It includes photographs and a QuickTime movie of embryonic stem cells growing in culture. http://www.news.wisc.edu/packages/stemcells. Accessed on December 1, 2004.

9

THE RICE THAT SAVES EYES

INGO POTRYKUS AND GOLDEN RICE

Every year, some 500,000 children in the developing world go blind and about a million die from infections because their diets lack a single vital nutrient: vitamin A. Two German-born scientists, one working in Switzerland and the other in Germany, announced in 1999 that they had invented a way to bring more vitamin A into the diets of people who need it. Their reward was to find themselves in the middle of a tug-of-war between biotechnology companies, which hyped their work as a cure-all for malnutrition, and groups that regarded genetic engineering, especially of food, as a potential destroyer of human health and the environment.

Experience with Hunger

Ingo Potrykus, the experimental team's head scientist, knew all too well how hunger felt. Born on December 5, 1933, in Hirschberg, Germany, he had grown up during World War II. His father, a doctor, was killed near the end of the war, and after Germany's defeat, Potrykus and his brothers "had to beg, steal and scrounge for food," *New York Times* reporter Jon Christensen wrote in an article about Potrykus published on November 21, 2000.

Perhaps this painful experience drew Potrykus to do research on food plants. After studying biology at the University of Cologne,

Ingo Potrykus developed a genetically altered form of rice that supporters say can combat a common form of malnutrition in developing countries, but critics claim that biotechnology companies benefit more from the rice than poor people ever will. (Ingo Potrykus)

he obtained his Ph.D. in plant genetics in 1968 from the Max Planck Institute for Plant Breeding Research, also in Cologne. He worked for several years at the University of Hohenheim, and then established a small laboratory at the Max Planck Institute for Plant Genetics in Ladenburg/Heidelberg, Germany, in the mid-1970s. He moved to a larger laboratory, consisting of three research groups, at the Friedrich Miescher Institute in Basel, Switzerland, in 1976 and earned his habilitation in botany, an advanced degree, from the University of Basel in 1982.

Potrykus joined the Swiss Federal Institute of Technology in Zurich (ETHZ), where he would spend the rest of his career, as a full professor in 1986. Within this large organization he and another professor established a new section, the Institute of Plant Sciences, which focused on the use of genetic engineering technology to increase food supplies in developing countries. (The first genetically engineered plants had been created in 1982.)

A Missing Vitamin

Potrykus's laboratory began a major program to alter genes in rice, the chief food of more than 40 percent of the world's people, around 1990. A diet consisting mostly of rice can contribute to the malnutrition that shortens the lives and ruins the health of so many of the world's poor because white rice, the type that most people prefer to eat, contains very few nutrients. White rice has been milled, or polished, to remove

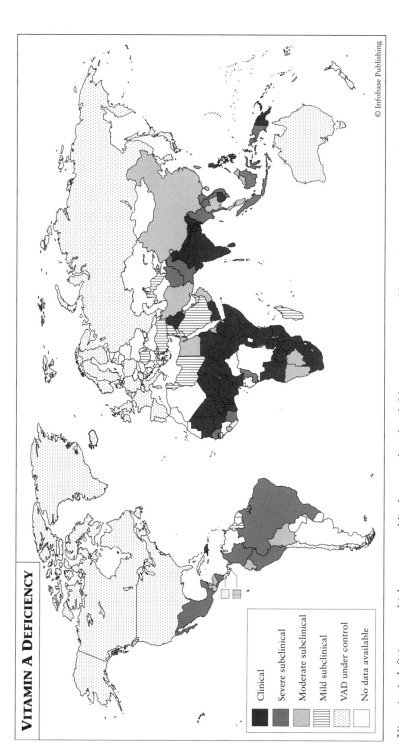

VITAMIN A DEFICIENCY

Clinical

Severe subclinical

Moderate subclinical

Mild subclinical

VAD under control

No data available

Vitamin A deficiency, which can cause blindness and make children more susceptible to infection, is common in many parts of the developing world and some parts of the developed world as well. This map shows levels from vitamin A deficiency in different parts of the world in the early 2000s.

the grain's brown outer husks, leaving only the starchy part called the endosperm. Potrykus hoped that if he used genetic engineering to add nutrients to rice endosperm, the improved grain would reduce malnutrition in Asia and other places where rice is a staple food.

Vitamin A, necessary for healthy eyes, skin, and immune systems, is among the nutrients missing from white rice. Green, leafy vegetables and certain other foods contain the vitamin or substances from which the human body can make it, but people whose diets lack these foods may suffer from vitamin A deficiency. The World Health Organization has estimated that vitamin A deficiency affects about 400 million people worldwide, including 124 million children, and contributes to the deaths of more than a million children yearly by making them more vulnerable to infections. This form of malnutrition is also the most important cause of preventable blindness among children in developing countries, making about 500,000 children sightless each year.

The Rockefeller Foundation, a large charitable organization in the United States, had a program that sponsored biotechnology research on rice, and Gary Toenniessen, the foundation's director of food security, agreed to fund part of Potrykus's work. Toenniessen suggested that Potrykus try to make rice endosperm produce a yellowish pigment called beta-carotene, which gives carrots and yellow corn their color, because the human body can convert this substance to vitamin A.

Perfect Partners

In 1992, Toenniessen invited Potrykus and other scientists to New York to discuss possible ways to engineer beta-carotene into rice. At this conference Potrykus met another German scientist, Peter Beyer of Freiburg University, who was trying to isolate the genes that allow daffodils to make beta-carotene. Potrykus stated in the October 2000 issue of *AgBioView* that Beyer was "the perfect partner" for his own research. The two men decided to cooperate in applying Beyer's discoveries about daffodil genes to Potrykus's rice, and Toenniessen said he would support their project.

The proposal seemed daunting indeed. Rice endosperm would need to produce three new proteins in order to make beta-carotene, which meant that three genes would have to be introduced into the plant and persuaded to function together. Inserting even one gene into a plant and making it operate normally was still extremely difficult. Potrykus wrote in *AgBioView* that almost no one, including Beyer and most of the Rockefeller officials, thought there was any hope of introducing three. Only Potrykus himself, with what he called the "ignorance and naiveté" of his "simple engineering mind," believed from the beginning that it could be done.

For most of the seven years after the project began in 1993, the naysayers appeared to be right. Beyer's group isolated the necessary genes—two from daffodils and one from a bacterium—but all of the Potrykus laboratory's attempts to force the genes into the rice genome failed. Finally, in 1998, Xudong Ye, a new postdoctoral student in Potrykus's laboratory, thought of a new approach. Much as other researchers had inserted genes into viruses and used the viruses to transfer the genes into animal cells, Ye put the three beta-carotene genes and DNA sequences called promoters, which would activate the genes, into a type of bacterium that infects plants. This bacterium, *Agrobacterium tumefaciens,* had been used in other plant genetic engineering experiments, but it had seldom succeeded in putting functional genes into rice or other cereal plants. Ye, however, made it work.

Genetic Breakthrough

Potrykus sent some of Ye's plants to Beyer in late 1998, and one night in February 1999, Beyer put grains from the plants in a polishing machine to remove their outer husks. When he removed the rice from the machine, he saw with excitement that the grains were not the usual white, but rather a pale yellow. Chemical analysis confirmed that the endosperm of the rice contained beta-carotene, and Beyer e-mailed Potrykus to tell him that the experiment was a success.

Ye formally presented his results on March 31, 1999, at a symposium honoring Potrykus on the occasion of Potrykus's mandatory retirement from the Swiss institute at age 65. Potrykus wrote in *AgBioView* that Ye's work was "a scientific breakthrough" because multiple genes, coding for a whole metabolic pathway, had never been engineered into a plant before.

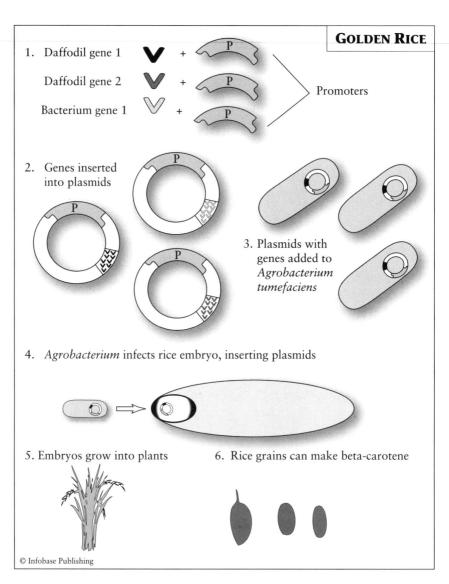

1. Daffodil gene 1 + P

   Daffodil gene 2 + P

   Bacterium gene 1 + P

   } Promoters

2. Genes inserted into plasmids

3. Plasmids with genes added to *Agrobacterium tumefaciens*

4. *Agrobacterium* infects rice embryo, inserting plasmids

5. Embryos grow into plants

6. Rice grains can make beta-carotene

© Infobase Publishing

To create golden rice, Ingo Potrykus and Peter Beyer's research teams isolated two genes from daffodils and one from a bacterium that, together, made possible the production of beta-carotene. They then added promoters (segments of DNA that turn genes on) to these genes (step 1). The scientists inserted the gene-promoter combinations into plasmids, circular combinations of genes in bacteria (step 2). They put the plasmids into Agrobacterium tumefaciens, a type of bacterium that infects plants (step 3). When the bacteria infected embryos (seeds) of rice plants, the bacteria inserted the beta-carotene genes into the plant cells (step 4). The seeds grew into rice plants. Because the grains from these plants carried the added genes, the grains could make beta-carotene (step 5).

Following the suggestion of a Thai business acquaintance, Potrykus and Beyer named their new plant "golden rice." They sent an article about it to *Nature,* the best-known scientific journal in Europe. In the cover letter that Potrykus sent with the manuscript, he pointed out that the plant's development was important for more than scientific reasons. A fierce debate was taking place worldwide about the value and possible dangers of genetically modified organisms (GMO) in foods, and golden rice, Potrykus said, offered a "timely and important demonstration of positive achievements of the GMO technology." *Nature,* however, rejected the manuscript. "We got the impression that *Nature* was more interested in cases which . . . question instead of support the value of genetic engineering technology," Potrykus complained in *AgBioView.*

A Mushrooming Industry

While Potrykus and Beyer were struggling with their rice plants in the late 1990s, agricultural biotechnology had gone from an experimental science to a major industry. In 1996, when crops containing altered genes were first grown commercially in the United States, only 4 million acres were planted with genetically modified seeds, but by 1998 the figure had risen to 10 times that. In 1999, when Potrykus's laboratory was ready to publicize the creation of golden rice, more than 50 genetically altered crops, including at least 24 food crops, had been approved for sale in the United States. Worldwide, 100 million acres were planted with such crops, and half the world's supply of soybeans and about a third of its corn were genetically engineered.

Not everyone welcomed genetically engineered crops, however. Opposition was especially strong in Europe, where genetically modified foods were often called Frankenfoods because people feared that genetic engineers, like the scientist in *Frankenstein,* Mary Shelley's 1818 novel, had created dangerous monsters. Organizations including Greenpeace, the Union of Concerned Scientists, and Jeremy Rifkin's Foundation on Economic Trends warned that the modified crops might pose threats to the environment if the crops' added

Certain types of genetically modified crops have become common in the United States and some other parts of the world. Most of the cotton and soybeans grown in the United States are now genetically altered, for example. The following figures show the growth of some common genetically engineered crops in the United States in recent years.

Year	Percentage of Soybeans Genetically Engineered	Percentage of Cotton Genetically Engineered	Percentage of Corn Genetically Engineered
2001	68%	69%	26%
2002	75%	71%	34%
2003	81%	73%	40%
2004	85%	76%	45%

genes were carried to wild plants in wind-blown pollen. Genetically modified foods might damage human health if people became allergic to them, the groups claimed. Some protesters went so far as to uproot engineered plants in test fields, just as others had done when the first genetically altered organisms to be tested outdoors, a type of bacteria, were sprayed on plants in 1987. Fearing such an attack, the Potrykus group conducted its last tests of golden rice in a greenhouse outside Zurich that had been built to withstand even hand grenades.

Child Saver or Fool's Gold?

Peter Raven of the Missouri Botanical Garden in St. Louis heard about Potrykus and Ye's work and was impressed. Raven arranged for Potrykus to describe golden rice at an international botanical congress and a press conference in August 1999. He also urged Potrykus's group to submit a technical paper on the rice to *Science,* the best-known science journal in the United States.

Science published the Swiss laboratory's paper on January 14, 2000. The same issue that carried the paper contained a commentary article by Mary Lou Guerinot of Dartmouth College's Department of Biological Sciences, which called the Potrykus group's achievement "a technical tour de force" that "exemplifies the best that agricultural biotechnology has to offer." Guerinot expressed the hope "that this application of plant genetic engineering to ameliorate human misery without regard to short-term profit will restore this technology to political acceptability."

With European protests cutting into its future business, the biotechnology industry strongly hoped the same thing. Indeed, Daniel Charles wrote in *Lords of the Harvest,* a book about the development of agricultural biotechnology, "defenders of biotechnology seized upon this innovation as if it were a rope thrown to drowning sailors." Biotech executives became even happier when *Time* ran a cover story on golden rice on July 31, 2000, claiming that "this rice could save a million kids a year." Large agricultural biotechnology companies such as the St. Louis–based Monsanto Company followed this favorable publicity with television commercials that featured smiling Asian children and shimmering rice paddies.

The other side of the war over genetically modified food quickly fired back. A February 2001 press release from Greenpeace denounced golden rice as "fool's gold" and claimed that the plant produced so little beta-carotene that a person would have to eat 20 pounds (9 kg) of cooked rice a day to obtain the minimum recommended daily allowance of vitamin A. A more probable daily rice serving of 0.7 pounds (300 g), the organization said, would provide only 8 percent of the amount needed each day. Greenpeace also pointed out that the human body can make vitamin A from beta-carotene only if the diet also contains fats, which many poor people's diets do not.

Indian activist Vandana Shiva, another foe of genetically engineered crops, said that attention given to golden rice obscured

PARALLELS: FROZEN TESTS FOR AN ICE-FIGHTING BACTERIUM

When frost (ice crystals) forms on the leaves of plants in winter, the plants may be severely damaged. Farmers try to prevent the formation of frost by covering or warming crops such as orange trees, but such methods are not always successful. In the 1970s, frost damage to crop plants cost U.S. farmers up to $1.5 billion a year.

In 1975, Steven Lindow, a plant pathologist (scientist who studies plant diseases) at the University of California, Berkeley, discovered that a protein on the surface of a common type of bacteria called *Pseudomonas syringae* helps ice crystals form on leaves. He also found a mutated form of the bacteria that lacked the gene for the ice-forming protein. Lindow reasoned that if he could make more of these "ice-minus" bacteria and spray them on plants, the altered bacteria might temporarily outcompete the normal ones and protect the plants against frost damage.

Lindow and his coworkers used genetic engineering to remove the ice-forming gene from normal *Pseudomonas* bacteria. The resulting ice-minus bacteria were effective in greenhouse tests, so in 1982, Lindow applied to the Recombinant DNA Advisory Committee (RAC) for permission to test the altered bacteria outdoors. If allowed to take place, Lindow's tests would be the first to release genetically modified organisms into the environment.

Jeremy Rifkin, president of the Foundation on Economic Trends and a foe of genetic engineering since the science's beginning, heard about the proposed tests and gathered supporters, including environmental groups and some scientists, to oppose it. The groups expressed fears that the engineered bacteria would spread into the environment and replace the normal form of *Pseudomonas,* upsetting the balance of ecosystems. In a 1984 article in *California Magazine,* Paul Ciotti wrote that Rifkin called the tests "ecological roulette."

Lawsuits filed by Rifkin and others delayed Lindow's tests for five years, but the RAC finally gave its approval. In spring 1987, just before the tests were scheduled to occur, protesters broke into the test fields and uprooted the strawberry and potato plants that were to be sprayed with the bacteria. Lindow and his fellow scientists replanted them, however, and the tests went forward. The bacteria protected the plants against frost and did not spread beyond the treated fields.

simpler and better ways of fighting vitamin A deficiency that were already in use, such as distributing vitamin supplements and encouraging poor people to raise and eat fruits and vegetables that contain vitamin A or substances that the body can convert into the vitamin. Most important, Shiva and other critics said, golden rice or any other proposed high-technology solution to world hunger ignored hunger's real causes, which the commentators held to be poverty, war, lack of land, and lack of access to a nutritious and diverse diet. Increasing the quantity or quality of food would not solve these problems, they warned. The critics even claimed that golden rice's only real purpose was to provide positive publicity for biotechnology companies and persuade people to accept genetically modified foods.

Center of a Storm

Like Ian Wilmut and James Thomson before him, Ingo Potrykus found himself the center of a media storm. Greenpeace and others sometimes attacked him personally, claiming that he was nothing more than a dupe, knowing or unknowing, of the biotechnology industry. Potrykus, in turn, wrote in an article defending golden rice in the March 2001 issue of *Plant Physiology* that "in my view, the Greenpeace management has but one real interest: to organize media-effective actions for fund raising." Because groups like Greenpeace were trying to deny a potentially valuable technology to the people who needed it most, he said, they should "be held responsible for the foreseeable unnecessary death and blindness of millions of poor every year." At the same time, Potrykus told Danish writer Gitte Meyer, "I don't want to become a part of PR campaigns for the [biotech] companies." He criticized biotechnology supporters for implying that golden rice was ready for widespread distribution, which he knew was not true.

Potrykus also tried to answer his critics' complaints. He admitted that golden rice, at least in the form it which it existed at that time, could provide only a small part of the recommended daily amount of vitamin A. However, he said, even this portion might be enough to prevent blindness and immune system defects. Furthermore, he pointed out, he had never claimed that golden rice could or should be people's only source of vitamin A, let alone a complete answer to malnutrition.

Golden Contract

Attacks from environmental groups were by no means Ingo Potrykus's only problem. From the beginning of his research, he and the governments and private charities that had provided his funding (which included the Swiss government, the U.S. National Science Foundation, and the European Union as well as the Rockefeller Foundation) had wanted to make golden rice available free to all poor people who wanted it, but he found that that decision might not be his to make. A patent search commissioned by the Rockefeller Foundation revealed that the making of golden rice involved 70 different patents (for genes, processes, and so on) belonging to 32 different companies and universities, including all the large multinational companies involved in agricultural biotechnology. Some patent holders were willing to allow free use of their technology for humanitarian purposes, but others were not.

Dealing with this tangled legal situation was too much for two private individuals, Potrykus and Beyer concluded. Instead, they decided that they "urgently needed a powerful partner" to negotiate on their behalf, as Potrykus wrote in *Plant Physiology*. They licensed their own patents to Greenovation, a small German company, which in turn brokered them to Zeneca, the agricultural division of the large British drug company AstraZeneca.

In the agreement that Potrykus's group made with Zeneca in May 2000, the company received the right to sell golden rice commercially in developed countries such as the United States and Japan. In return, it promised to give golden rice seeds free to all farmers who earned less than $10,000 from growing and selling the rice. Zeneca also agreed to obtain the necessary permissions from other patent holders, to conduct the environmental and health safety tests that governments would require before permitting the rice to be grown, and to allow Potrykus and Beyer to give the rice or other plants with the same inserted genes to nonprofit research institutions that wanted to develop the plants further or crossbreed them with local varieties. With the cooperation of Zeneca, Potrykus and Beyer established the Golden Rice Humanitarian Board to oversee further research on the rice and the grain's eventual distribution.

As with the value of the rice itself, opinions differed about Potrykus's arrangement with Zeneca. Some saw it as a good blueprint for future agreements between scientists and biotechnology corporations. On the other hand, an anti-GMO group called GRAIN (Genetic Resources Action International) wrote in February 2001 that "the deal with AstraZeneca . . . not only surrendered a decade of publicly funded research to commercial control, but—more importantly—it strengthened the North's [developed countries'] patent hegemony [domination] worldwide."

Testing Underway

Ingo Potrykus was well aware that, even if no one had opposed golden rice, his discovery was far from ready for widespread use. Golden rice had not been planted in large quantities or tested outdoors, so no one knew how hardy it would be in farmers' fields. Although Potrykus thought that the rice would be unlikely to harm either the environment or human health, he knew that many years of testing would be necessary to prove the rice's safety.

Beginning in January 2001, Potrykus's Golden Rice Board has been collaborating with the International Rice Research Institute in the Philippines and 13 other rice research institutions in India, China, Indonesia, and elsewhere to carry out these tests. Golden rice belongs to a species that does not grow well in tropical climates, where many developing countries are located, so the institutes are also crossbreeding the rice with other rice varieties that will be more useful in the developing world. The first field trials and harvest of golden rice in the United States were completed in September 2004, and commercial production of the rice expected to begin in India around 2009.

ISSUES: PATENTING LIVING THINGS

In 1793, the U.S. Congress passed a law stating that "any new and useful art, machine, manufacture, or composition of matter" (the word *art* was changed to *process* in 1952) could be patented. A patent gives an inventor the exclusive rights to an invention's use and sale for a limited period, in exchange for the inventor's publishing the details of his or her invention. The U.S. Supreme Court ruled in 1980 that living things could be patented if human beings had altered them. The first patent for a genetically altered plant was issued in 1985. Critics say that allowing living things to be patented gives biotechnology companies too much power, but the companies claim that patent protection is necessary for them to recover the high cost of developing genetically engineered organisms, which may benefit humanity.

Ingo Potrykus had mixed feelings about the patent's effect on golden rice. He wrote in the October 23, 2000, issue of *AgBioView*:

It seemed to me unacceptable, even immoral, that an achievement based on research in a public institution and with exclusively public funding, and designed for a humanitarian purpose, was in the hands of those who had patented enabling technology early enough. . . . It turned out that whatever public research one was doing, it was all in the hands of industry (and some universities). At that time [when he discovered that patents could restrict distribution of the rice] I was much tempted to join those who radically fight patenting.

After thinking the matter over, however, Potrykus reconsidered:

I . . . became aware that "Golden Rice" development was only possible because there was patenting. Much of the technology I had been using was publicly known because the inventors could protect their right. Much of it would have remained secret [without patents]. . . . If we are interested to use all the knowledge to the benefit of the poor, it does not make sense to fight against patenting. It makes far more sense to fight for a sensible use of intellectual property rights.

Since his retirement from ETHZ, Potrykus has spent most of his time explaining golden rice's advantages to the public and helping to oversee its testing and distribution. He has received several awards for his work, including the Kumho Science International Award in Plant Molecular Biology and Biotechnology (2000), the European Culture Award in Science, and the American Society of Plant Biologists' Leadership in Science Public Service Award (2001).

Beyer and others, meanwhile, are trying to increase the amount of beta-carotene the rice makes and to add other nutrients to the grain, including iron, which is also absent from many poor people's diets. In early 2005, Syngenta announced development of a new strain of golden rice that contains up to 23 times more beta-carotene than the original strain. In addition, researchers are exploring ways to engineer beta-carotene production into other crops commonly eaten by poor people in the developing world, including wheat, cassava, sweet potatoes, and bananas.

No one knows how useful golden rice, or any genetically engineered crop, will prove to be in the long run. Critics such as Greenpeace and Vandana Shiva are surely correct that hunger and malnutrition are too complex a problem to be solved merely by technology, let alone by any single invention. Unless some unforeseen danger from the plant is revealed, however, Potrykus and his supporters see little reason why golden rice should not contribute whatever it can.

Chronology

1933	Ingo Potrykus born in Hirschberg, Germany, on December 5
1968	Potrykus obtains Ph.D. from Max Planck Institute for Plant Breeding Research
1976	Potrykus joins Friedrich Miescher Institute in Basel, Switzerland
1982	Potrykus earns Habilitation in Botany from University of Basel
	First genetically engineered plants created

1986	Potrykus joins Swiss Federal Institute of Technology in Zurich (ETHZ) and cofounds the Institute of Plant Sciences
1990	Potrykus's laboratory begins research aimed at altering genes in rice
	Rockefeller Foundation agrees to supply part of Potrykus's funding
1992	Potrykus meets Peter Beyer of Freiburg University at a Rockefeller Foundation symposium and decides to work with him
1993	Potrykus and Beyer begin project to insert multiple genes needed to make beta-carotene, a precursor of vitamin A, into rice
1996	Crops containing altered genes first grown commercially in the United States
1998	Xudong Ye uses bacteria to insert three genes into rice, enabling the endosperm of the rice grains to make beta-carotene
1999	On March 31, Ye announces the success of his rice work, and Potrykus retires from ETHZ
	Potrykus describes golden rice at an international botanical congress and a press conference in August
2000	Scientific paper describing golden rice appears in the January 14 issue of *Science*
	In May, Potrykus and Beyer work out a licensing agreement for golden rice with British agricultural biotechnology company Zeneca
	A cover story on golden rice appears in the July 31 issue of *Time*
2001	International Rice Research Institute begins testing golden rice in the Philippines in January
	In February, Greenpeace calls golden rice "fool's gold"
2004	First field trials of golden rice in the United States are completed in September
2005	New strain of golden rice containing is more beta-carotene than 23 times the original one developed

Further Reading

Books

Charles, Daniel. *Lords of the Harvest: Biotech, Big Money, and the Future of Food.* Cambridge, Mass: Perseus Books, 2002.
    Describes the development of genetically engineered crops, with an emphasis on the role of large multinational companies, especially Monsanto.
Pringle, Peter. *Food, Inc.: Mendel to Monsanto—The Promises and Perils of the Biotech Harvest.* New York: Simon and Schuster, 2003.
    History and evaluation of agricultural biotechnology includes a chapter on golden rice.

Articles

Christensen, Jon. "Golden Rice in a Grenade-Proof Greenhouse." *New York Times,* 21 November 2000, pp. D1, F1.
    Profile of Potrykus provides background on his work.
Ciotti, Paul. "Saving Mankind from the Great Potato Menace," *California Magazine,* October 1984, pp. 97–98.
    Describes opposition to Steven Lindow's proposed test of "ice-minus" bacteria, the first test that would release genetically modified organisms into the environment.
"Genetically Engineered 'Golden Rice' Is Fool's Gold." Greenpeace. Posted February 9, 2001. Available online. URL: http://archive. greenpeace.org/pressreleases/geneng/2001feb9.html. Accessed on May 4, 2006.
    Explains why the organization feels that golden rice will have little effect on vitamin A deficiency.
"Grains of Delusion: Golden Rice Seen from the Ground." GRAIN (Genetic Resources Action International). Posted February 2001. Available online. URL: http://www.grain.org/briefings/?id=18. Accessed on May 4, 2006.
    Detailed criticism of the value of golden rice and the motives of those who produced it.
Guerinot, Mary Lou. "The Green Revolution Strikes Gold," *Science,* 14 January 2000, p. 241.

Commentary article praising golden rice, accompanying the scientific paper in which the rice's creation is described.

"Ingo Potrykus." GM Watch. Available online. URL: http://www. gmwatch.org/profile.asp?page=P. Accessed on May 4, 2006.
Critical biographical sketch of Potrykus, portraying him as a major force in the biotechnology industry's attempts to overstate the value of golden rice to the developing world.

Meyer, Gitte. "A Long Journey Ahead for Golden Rice." Danish Centre for Bioethics and Risk Assessment. Posted June 2001. Available online. URL: http://www.bioethics.kvl.dk/tekster/git-golden.PDF. Accessed on May 4, 2006.
Includes quotes from Ingo Potrykus and from Benny Haerlin of Greenpeace.

Nash, J. Madeleine. "Grains of Hope," *Time,* 31 July 2000, pp. 14–22.
This article, which made the general public aware of golden rice, stresses the engineered crop's advantages but also describes critics' concerns.

Potrykus, Ingo. "Golden Rice and Beyond," *Plant Physiology* 125 (March 2001): 1157–1161.
Addresses issues about golden rice raised by opponents of agricultural biotechnology and genetically engineered foods.

———. "The 'Golden Rice' Tale," *AgBioView,* 2 October 2000.
Potrykus's detailed account of the research that produced golden rice. Article includes some biographical background and discussion of the sociopolitical issues raised by the rice and opposition to it. Somewhat difficult reading.

Shiva, Vandana. "Genetically Engineered Vitamin 'A' Rice: A Blind Approach to Blindness Prevention." Posted February 14, 2000. Available online. URL: http://www.biotech-info.net/blind_rice. html. Accessed on May 4, 2006.
The Indian activist, a strong opponent of genetic engineering, describes possible risks associated with golden rice and recommends alternative approaches to reducing vitamin A deficiency.

Ye, Xudong, et al. "Engineering the Provitamin A ([Beta]-Carotene) Biosynthetic Pathway into (Carotenoid-Free) Rice Endosperm." *Science,* 14 January 2000, p. 303.
Scientific paper announcing the production of golden rice.

Web Sites

AgBioTech InfoNet. Extensive site about applications of genetic engineering to agriculture and the effects and implications of the technology presents papers both favoring and criticizing genetic engineering. Reprints of numerous articles attacking and defending golden rice can be found at http://www.biotech-info.net/golden. html. Accessed on September 15, 2004.

10

THE GENOME RACE

FRANCIS COLLINS, CRAIG VENTER, AND SEQUENCING THE HUMAN GENOME

Francis Collins led the international Human Genome Project, which determined the base sequence of the complete collection of genes in human beings. (National Human Genome Research Institute)

The Human Genome Project (HGP) has often been compared to the giant 1960s program that first took human beings to the Moon. Instead of exploring a body in space, however, the HGP's purpose was to reach inside the human body and describe, letter by genetic letter, the coded blueprint for humanity itself: the sequence of bases in the entire human genome. In the ceremony marking the completion of the sequence's first draft on June 26, 2000, President Bill Clinton called this genetic list "the most important, most wondrous map ever produced by humankind."

Like the space program that led to the Moon landing, the effort to sequence the human genome was often called a race—not between countries, like the earlier "space race" between the United States and the Soviet Union, but between groups of scientists. Although many of those involved say that the media exaggerated the "race" aspect, the genome sequencing project certainly became a competition, not only between sets of people but between sponsors and styles of science: public versus private, national versus international, nonprofit versus for-profit. The two men who led the competing teams, Francis Collins and Craig Venter, exemplified those differences—but they also had much in common, including some of the reasons for their success.

"Big Science"

The Human Genome Project began long before either Collins or Venter had any part in it. Robert Sinsheimer, chancellor of the University of California at Santa Cruz, first proposed working out the base sequence of all the molecules in a human being's DNA at a conference in May 1985. At the time, most scientists thought the idea impractical or perhaps even impossible. The best laboratories could sequence only about 1,000 base pairs a day, and the human genome was thought to contain a little more than 3 billion such pairs.

Nonetheless, the goal was so inspiring that it began to gather supporters. The U.S. Department of Energy (DOE) was among the first. One of the department's jobs was to investigate health risks produced by nuclear energy, and Charles DeLisi, then director of DOE's Office of Health and Environmental Research, thought that knowing the full sequence of a normal human genome would help the department identify radiation-caused mutations. In 1986, therefore, DeLisi announced that DOE would fund research on mapping and sequencing the human genome. James Wyngaarden, then head of the National Institutes of Health (NIH), and James Watson, codiscoverer of DNA's structure, also became enthusiastic about a possible sequencing project.

The Human Genome Project began in 1989, with Watson as its first director. The project was expected to cost $3 billion and take 15 years. It would be a publicly funded, international endeavor, although the United States would be in charge of it and do more than half the work. The genome project was biology's first venture into "Big Science," the kind of gigantic, multigovernment effort that had marked physicists' exploration of the inside of the atom. It eventually involved 16 sequencing centers in the United States, Britain, France, Germany, Japan, and China.

HUMAN GENOME CENTERS

UNITED STATES

Walnut Creek, California
Stanford, California
Seattle, Washington
Houston, Texas
Dallas, Texas
St. Louis, Missouri
Cambridge, Massachusetts
Waltham, Massachusetts
Cold Spring Harbor, New York

BRITAIN (UNITED KINGDOM)

Hinxton, Cambridgeshire

CHINA

Beijing

FRANCE

Evry

GERMANY
Braunschweig
Jena
Berlin

JAPAN
Tokyo

Gene Hunter

James Watson left the Human Genome Project in 1992 after a disagreement with Bernadine Healy, then head of the National Institutes of Health. Healy wanted a new director who, like Watson, was a highly respected scientist who could lead, coordinate, and inspire the many different groups working on the project. The person she chose was Francis Collins. "Collins was an excellent choice," Watson wrote in his book on the history of late 20th-century genetics, *DNA: The Secret of Life.*

Heading a historic international project surely must have been far from Francis Sellers Collins's dreams as he grew up on a 95-acre farm in the Shenandoah Valley of Virginia with no indoor plumbing. Born in Staunton, Virginia, on April 14, 1950, Collins thought at first more about drama and music than science, because those were his parents' interests. His mother wrote plays, and his father, a drama professor at a nearby women's college, staged them in a theater that the couple built on their farm. Collins himself wrote and directed his own dramatic version of *The Wizard of Oz* when he was just seven years old, and he learned to play several instruments. His parents educated him at home until sixth grade, by which time he was academically two years ahead of other students his age.

Turning away from the arts as he grew up, Collins somehow became attracted to science. At first he preferred mathematics and physics to biology, which he saw as chaotic and unpredictable. He earned a B.S. in chemistry at the University of Virginia in 1970 and a Ph.D. in physical chemistry from Yale University in 1974. A biochemistry course at Yale, however, made Collins decide that biology might be worth his attention after all. He especially liked genetics, which "was so elegant, so principle-based, so digital, so mathemati-cal," as he said to Dana Wilkie in an interview published in *The Scientist* on September 3, 2001.

Leaving physics behind, Collins attended medical school at the University of North Carolina and earned his M.D. in 1977. His specialty was medical genetics, the study of genes that cause or con-tribute to disease. While doing postdoctoral work in this subject at Yale in the early 1980s, he developed a technique called positional cloning, which speeded up the process of finding disease-causing genes by five to 10 times. Instead of "walking" slowly along a piece of DNA looking for markers related to a gene, a scientist using Collins's method could "jump" across larger stretches.

Collins joined the University of Michigan, Ann Arbor, as an assis-tant professor in 1984, heading a laboratory that looked for genes linked to inherited illnesses. There, working with a Canadian research group led by Taiwanese-born researcher Lap-Chee Tsui, Collins used his positional cloning technique to codiscover the gene responsible for cystic fibrosis in 1989. Cystic fibrosis affects one in every 2,000 children, making them prone to infections that damage their lungs, and usually leads to an early death. Collins also discovered genes that cause several rarer diseases, and he played a major part in finding the gene for Huntington's disease, the inherited illness that afflicted Nancy Wexler's family.

Herding Cats

Managing the huge Human Genome Project required a special kind of leadership skill, and when Francis Collins took over the project's directorship in 1993, he showed that he possessed it. Collins became known for his ability to persuade the many, often contentious groups of scientists involved in the HGP to cooperate, a process that Craig Venter, later to be Collins's rival, described to Tim Stevens of *Industry Week* as "herding cats." Quoted in the same article, Aristides (Ari) Patrinos, associate director of the Department of Energy's Office of Science, said that "Collins . . . has an incredible ability to lead large groups of people." Collins used a "bottom-up" management style, seeking opinions and building consensus through techniques such as setting up weekly telephone conference calls with the leaders of the major sequencing centers.

During the early 1990s, the HGP focused on improving technology to make sequencing faster, less expensive, and more automated. Researchers also began mapping the human genome to find landmarks that could guide later sequencers. Around 1995, centers also started sequencing the genomes of simpler organisms heavily studied by geneticists, such as the nematode *Caenorhabditis elegans*. Knowing about these organisms' genes would be valuable in itself and would provide material against which the human genome could be compared.

Craig Venter, cofounder of Celera Genomics, claimed in 1998 that this private company would sequence the human genome more quickly and cheaply than the government-sponsored project. (Venter Institute)

Then in May 1998, when only 3 percent of the human genome had been sequenced, the HGP suffered what James Watson, in *DNA: The Secret of Life,* called "the molecular biological equivalent of an earthquake." A newly formed private company, Celera Genomics Corporation, announced that it would sequence the human genome by 2001—four years before the HGP's 2005 deadline—and would do the job more cheaply as well.

Conversion in Vietnam

The man behind Celera's challenge was the company's president and chief scientific officer, John Craig Venter. Francis Collins's fondness for leather jackets and his Honda Nighthawk 750 motorcycle might give him a slightly controversial image outside the laboratory, but scientific and media perceptions of Venter as a "bad boy" ran much deeper.

Venter had been born on October 14, 1946, in Salt Lake City, Utah. He grew up in the respectable San Francisco suburb of Millbrae, but respectability never interested him. He found school boring, and his grades were usually poor. When he graduated from high school, all he wanted was to be a surfer.

All that changed when Venter enlisted in the U.S. Navy and was sent to fight in Vietnam in the late 1960s. As a medical corpsman in Da Nang, he told Jocelyn Selim and David Ewing Duncan in an interview published in *Discover* in December 2004, he suddenly realized that "when I had specific knowledge, I could save people's lives." He decided that if he survived the war, he would become a physician and work in a developing country.

When Venter returned to the United States, he sped through studies at the University of California, San Diego, earning a bachelor's degree in biochemistry in 1972 and a doctorate in physiology and pharmacology in 1975. He said in the *Discover* interview that he "started making major science breakthroughs" and published his first scientific paper while still an undergraduate.

Like Francis Collins, Craig Venter became captivated by genetics and changed his focus from medicine to research. Skipping over the usual several years of postdoctoral study, Venter was given his own laboratory at the State University of New York, Buffalo, as soon as he finished his Ph.D. There he studied cell surface proteins called receptors, through which hormones and other substances in the body communicate with cells.

Shortcuts to Sequencing

Venter moved to the National Institutes of Health (NIH) in 1984 and became interested in determining the base sequence of genes that made receptor proteins. Impatient with the slow sequencing techniques most laboratories used and unable to persuade his superiors to buy one of the newly invented automated DNA sequencing machines, Venter used his own discretionary funds to purchase such a machine in 1986.

Venter went on to develop his own improvements in sequencing methods. The first improvement built on a technique that Venter learned from British molecular biologist Sydney Brenner around 1990. Only a small part of living things' genomes consists of functioning genes; the rest is DNA of seemingly random sequence, often called "junk DNA" because its function, if any, is unknown. When a cell prepares to make proteins, it copies only the DNA sequences it needs—the genes—into the messenger RNA that will direct protein manufacture. Messenger RNA thus represents most of the DNA that is active, or expressed, with the "junk" edited out. Using an enzyme from retroviruses, Brenner made segments of cells' messenger RNA into complementary DNA copies (cDNA), which could then be sequenced and matched against libraries of known genes. Venter and Mark Adams, one of Venter's postdoctoral students at NIH, found that they needed to sequence only a small part of each complementary DNA segment—about 500 bases' worth—in order to identify it. Using these expressed sequence tags, as Venter called them, along with a computer program to check them against gene libraries, Venter and Adams found hundreds of new genes in brain cells in 1990. At a time when only about 3,000 human genes of any kind were known, this was a startling feat.

Venter left NIH in 1992 and, with funding from venture capitalist Wallace Steinberg, established his own nonprofit research institute in Maryland, the Institute for Genomic Research (TIGR, pronounced "tiger"). There, Venter invented a second new sequencing technique, in which he broke genomes into many tiny fragments and had machines determine the fragments' sequence. He then used complex computer programs to put the sequences in order by identifying parts of them that overlapped. Meredith Wadman of *Fortune* magazine wrote that this method, which Venter called whole genome shotgun sequencing, was like chopping 20 encyclopedias into shreds and then reassembling them. Using the shotgun technique, Venter and Nobel Prize winner Hamilton Smith sequenced the first complete genome of a living thing in 1995. The genome, 1.8 million base pairs long, came from a bacterium called *Hemophilus influenzae,* which causes lung and brain infections.

Although the staff of TIGR was not nearly as large as the number of people working on the Human Genome Project, Craig Venter's successes at TIGR illustrated one feature that Venter has in common with Francis Collins: Both are exceptionally adept leaders. They pride themselves on choosing excellent scientists for their teams and inspiring them without micromanaging their activities. Instead of drawing

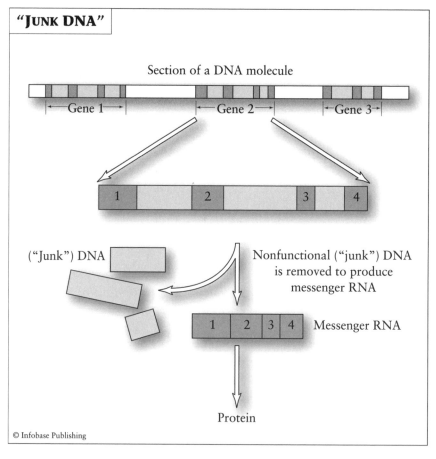

"JUNK DNA"

Section of a DNA molecule

Gene 1   Gene 2   Gene 3

1   2   3   4

("Junk") DNA

Nonfunctional ("junk") DNA is removed to produce messenger RNA

1 2 3 4   Messenger RNA

Protein

© Infobase Publishing

Large parts of a DNA molecule do not make proteins or perform any other known function, so some scientists call these segments "junk DNA." A cell does not copy these stretches when it makes the messenger RNA that carries the instructions for protein manufacture. Sydney Brenner made genome sequencing easier by making DNA copies of messenger RNA, eliminating the need to sequence the "junk." Craig Venter found out that only part of each DNA copy needed to be sequenced in order to identify genes.

SOLVING PROBLEMS: AUTOMATIC SEQUENCING MACHINES

Frederick Sanger of Britain's Cambridge University and Walter Gilbert of Harvard developed the first practical DNA sequencing methods in the mid-1970s, but their techniques were slow and very labor intensive. In the early 1980s, Michael Hunkapiller and Lloyd Smith, two scientists in the laboratory of Leroy Hood at the California Institute of Technology (Caltech), worked out a way to speed up Sanger's procedure and perform much of it automatically.

Hunkapiller and Smith labeled bases in DNA fragments with four different dyes that fluoresced, or glowed, under laser light—one dye for each type of base. Because the bases were color coded, all four types could be identified in a single test, whereas Sanger had had to run a separate test for each kind of base. This change alone therefore made the Sanger technique four times more efficient. An electric eye picked up the colors and sent the information about their pattern directly to a computer. Computers had sometimes been used to analyze tests done with Sanger's method, but data from the tests had to be typed in by hand, a very tedious and error-prone process.

In 1983, Hunkapiller joined Applied Biosystems, an instrument-making company owned by Perkin-Elmer Corporation, and Applied Biosystems began making the machines that he and Smith had designed. Craig Venter met Hunkapiller in the late 1980s, when Venter became enthusiastic about doing DNA sequencing by machine.

Sensing potential profit for his sequencing machine company and appealing to Venter's long-held desire to sequence the human genome, Hunkapiller invited Venter to join him in forming Celera Genomics Corporation in 1998. By then, Hunkapiller was making greatly improved sequencing machines. In the end, both Celera and the publicly funded Human Genome Project used Hunkapiller's machines.

plans out of team members' discussions as Collins has, however, Venter told Tim Stevens in December 2000, "I paint the overall vision, then turn [my scientists] loose and rely on their expertise."

Venter left TIGR in January 1998 and joined with Michael Hunkapiller, one of the inventors of the techniques behind automatic sequencing machines, to form a new company that they called Celera, the Latin word for "speed." Four months later, Celera issued its startling challenge to the Human Genome Project. The company planned to outrace the government project by combining Venter's shotgun sequencing method, 300 of Hunkapiller's state-of-the-art machines, and what James Watson (in *DNA: The Secret of Life*) called "the single greatest concentration of computing power outside the Pentagon."

Toward the Finish Line

Faced with competition and concerned that a private company might be able to control access to the human genome sequence, Francis Collins and the other Human Genome Project leaders rethought their goals and timeline. They decided that the government project would aim initially for a "working draft" covering 90 percent of the genome, rather than a complete sequence, and that it would complete this work by 2001, the same year Celera had named.

Several times during the next few years the government group and Celera tried to join forces, but their talks always broke down. The chief point of disagreement was the way that the genetic information being obtained would be published. Since 1996, the government project had posted all sequence data free in a publicly funded database on the Internet within 24 hours of its acquisition, with no restrictions on access to or use of the information. Venter agreed that the raw sequence data should be published, but he wanted commercial users to agree not to redistribute it. According to James Watson's *DNA: The Secret of Life*, Celera also planned to delay publishing its data for three months and sell subscriptions for advance viewing.

Most of the actual sequencing in the competing projects—not to mention the monumental computing task of putting all the individually sequenced pieces together in the correct order—took place in 1999 and early 2000, as both groups pushed toward a deadline, arrived at after consultation with the Clinton administration, of June 26, 2000, for completion of the initial sequence and analysis of the human genome. The administration also pressured Collins and Venter to make at least a temporary truce with one another. After a last-minute agreement brokered by Ari Patrinos, both leaders appeared with Clinton in the East Room of the White House for the announcement of the historic achievement (British prime minister Tony Blair joined them by satellite). The race, if such it was, was officially declared a tie.

Challenging Projects

Francis Collins and Craig Venter have maintained very active careers since their historic day at the White House. Collins still heads the National Human Genome Research Institute, as well as a laboratory at NIH that focuses on identifying disease genes. Collins's group announced in March 2004, for instance, that they had found variations in a certain gene that seem to be associated with increased risk of type 2 diabetes, a common and serious condition that often develops in older people who are overweight. Collins has been honored with many awards, including election to the National Academy of Sciences and, in 2003, the Secretary's Gold Award from the Department of Energy (DOE), the department's highest honorary award.

Venter, for his part, left Celera in January 2002. He founded a nonprofit institution, the J. Craig Venter Science Foundation, in October 2004, and a commercial enterprise, Synthetic Genomics, Inc., in June 2005. Like Collins, Venter has been elected to the National Academy of Sciences, and he has received other honors as well. The Institute for Scientific Information in Philadelphia, which ranks scientists according to the frequency with which other researchers cite their publications, places Venter in the top 0.05 percent of molecular biologists.

Venter's current projects are just as startling as his earlier ones. One project involves creating a synthetic bacterium by assembling from short stretches of DNA the 300 or so genes that seem to be necessary for life and inserting them into bacteria from which the

SOCIAL IMPACT: REVOLUTIONARY KNOWLEDGE

Whatever other disputes they might have had, Francis Collins and Craig Venter agree on the value of the Human Genome Project (HGP). In an interview with Lucinda M. O'Neill, published in *Exceptional Parent* in October 2002, for instance, Collins called the project "the most important organized scientific enterprise that humankind has ever undertaken."

Both leaders have said repeatedly that they expect the decoding of the human genome to revolutionize medicine. To begin with, knowledge of the genome sequence should greatly speed up the process of finding the genetic variations that cause inherited diseases or contribute to more common illnesses such as heart disease and cancer. Once scientists learn what genes, proteins, and processes are involved in particular diseases, they can design drugs that will correct defects or replace missing proteins without harming cells and causing side effects, as so many drugs do today. A few of these targeted drugs have already entered the market, and many more are being designed and tested.

Knowledge obtained from the genome project will also improve the way physicians treat individual patients, Collins and Venter believe. In a decade or two, they say, people will be able to receive complete

genetic material has been removed. Venter hopes to engineer this basic bacterium to be environmentally useful in various ways, for instance by cleaning up nuclear waste or generating hydrogen for use as a fuel.

Venter is also sailing his yacht, the *Sorcerer II*, around the world, collecting samples of ocean microorganisms every 200 miles and shipping them back to his institute for analysis by the shotgun technique. He has published results of a pilot project conducted in early 2003 in the Sargasso Sea off Bermuda, an area usually thought to contain relatively few types of organisms, in which his team found 1,800 new species and 1.2 million new genes—10 times the number of genes previously known in all species on Earth.

readouts of their individual genomes, perhaps at birth. Warned that they are at greater-than-average risk of developing particular health problems, individuals could take steps to prevent them. A person who inherits genes that increase the risk of cancer, for instance, might be tested often for the disease so it can be caught early. A person with genes that make a heart attack likely might try to reduce the risk by eating a healthy diet and exercising regularly. If a person has to be treated for a disease, the person's genetic profile will help a physician determine which drugs are likely to work best and cause the fewest side effects in that individual.

At the same time, Collins and Venter are concerned about misuse and misunderstanding of the genetic information they helped produce. (Indeed, genome scientists have worried about these problems since the Human Genome Project began. First 3 percent, and later 5 percent, of the HGP budget was devoted to a program that examined the ethical, legal, and social implications of the project and the information it generates.) The two men have strongly urged Congress to pass legislation that would bar insurance companies and employers from discriminating against people on the basis of their genetic makeup, for example. Venter and Collins also have warned people against assuming that genes determine everything about a person's health or behavior. Environmental factors and personal choice, the two scientists say, are just as important as genes in shaping an individual's life.

End and Beginning

In April 2003, on the 50th anniversary of the publication of James Watson and Francis Crick's paper revealing DNA's structure, the Human Genome Project announced the completion of a finished version of the human genome sequence. All the scientists involved in the sequencing know, however, that the crucial work of interpreting this mountain of data is just starting.

Genome analysts have already uncovered some surprises. Perhaps the most important one is the fact that human beings appear to have far fewer genes than scientists had assumed—less than 25,000 instead of the 100,000 that were predicted at the beginning of the genome project.

On the other hand, the genes appear to be more versatile than expected. For decades, scientists believed that each gene made only one protein, but they now know that many human genes can produce at least three. Whether they were pleased about sharing the credit or not, both Francis Collins and Craig Venter—and the hundreds of people working in the very different organizations that these two men headed—played important parts in decoding the human genome. Similarly, both public and private organizations, scientific team builders and risk-taking individualists, consensus builders and visionaries, are sure to be necessary to reap the fruit of this amazing endeavor in the future.

Chronology

1946	Craig Venter born in Salt Lake City, Utah, on October 14
1950	Francis Collins born in Staunton, Virginia, on April 14
1970s	In mid-decade, Frederick Sanger and Walter Gilbert invent the first practical DNA sequencing techniques
1974	Collins earns Ph.D. in physical chemistry from Yale University
1975	Venter earns Ph.D. in physiology and pharmacology from University of California, San Diego
1977	Collins earns M.D. from University of North Carolina
1980s	Early in the decade, Collins develops positional cloning, a technique that speeds up location of disease-causing genes Michael Hunkapiller and others develop automatic gene sequencing machines
1984	Collins joins University of Michigan, Ann Arbor Venter joins National Institutes of Health
1985	In May, Robert Sinsheimer proposes determining the base sequence of the entire human genome
1986	U.S. Department of Energy announces that it will fund research on mapping and sequencing the human genome

1989	Human Genome Project (HGP) begins, with James Watson as director
	Teams led by Francis Collins and Lap-Chee Tsui identify the gene that causes cystic fibrosis
1990	Venter and Mark Adams invent expressed sequence tag technique and use it to find hundreds of new genes in brain cells
1990s	HGP improves sequencing technology and begins to map human genome early in the decade
	Craig Venter invents whole genome shotgun sequencing
1992	James Watson resigns directorship of Human Genome Project
	With funding from venture capitalist Wallace Steinberg, Venter establishes the Institute for Genomic Research (TIGR) in Maryland
1993	Francis Collins takes over HGP directorship
1995	Venter's group sequences first genome of a living thing, bacterium *Hemophilus influenzae*
1998	In January, Venter leaves TIGR and, with Michael Hunkapiller, forms Celera Genomics Corporation
	In May, Celera announces that it will sequence the human genome by 2001, sooner and more cheaply than the HGP
1999–2000	Most sequencing of human genome and assembly of sequences in order takes place in public and private projects
2000	Accompanied by Collins and Venter, President Bill Clinton announces completion of a rough draft of the human DNA sequence in a White House ceremony on June 26
2002	In January, Venter leaves Celera and establishes three nonprofit research institutions
2003	In April, Human Genome Project leaders announce the completion of the final version of the human genome sequence on the 50th anniversary of the publication of Watson and Crick's paper describing the structure of DNA

2004	In March, the Collins laboratory announces identification of gene variations associated with increased risk of type 2 diabetes
	March, Venter publishes results of a 2003 project that sampled microorganisms from the Sargasso Sea and sequenced their genomes, discovering 1,800 new species and 1.2 million new genes

Further Reading

Books

Davies, Kevin. *Cracking the Genome*. New York: Free Press/Simon & Schuster, 2001.
> Recounts the advances in molecular biology that led to the Human Genome Project and the disagreements about technique and about control and use of genetic information that divided the public (government) and private (commercial) versions of the project.

Wade, Nicholas. *Life Script: How the Human Genome Discoveries Will Transform Medicine and Enhance Your Health*. New York: Touchstone Books, 2002.
> This book, primarily consisting of articles from the *New York Times*, describes the race to decipher the human genome and the likely medical and social effects that information about the genome will have.

Watson, James D. *DNA: The Secret of Life*. New York: Alfred A. Knopf, 2003.
> Contains a chapter on the Human Genome Project, including its beginnings and Watson's role in it.

Wickelgren, Ingrid. *The Gene Masters*. New York: Times Books/ Henry Holt, 2002.
> Description of the Human Genome Project that stresses the competition between the public project, headed by Francis Collins, and the private venture, headed by Craig Venter.

Articles

Collins, Francis, and Victor A. McKusick. "Implications of the Human Genome Project for Medical Science," *Journal of the American Medical Association* 285 (February 7, 2001): 540.

Describes the project, including its importance and work that remains to be done on it, and its implications for both experimental and mainstream medicine.

Golden, Frederic, and Michael D. Lemonick. "The Race Is Over," *Time*, 3 July 2000, pp. 12–17.

Describes the announcement of the completion of a rough draft of the human genome and the events that led up to it.

"International Consortium Completes Human Genome Project," *Genomics & Genetics Weekly* (May 9, 2003): 32.

The International Human Genome Sequencing Consortium announces the successful completion of a finished draft of the human genome more than two years ahead of the schedule proposed when the Human Genome Project began.

Kramer, David. "Q&A: Human Genome Research Institute Director Francis Collins," *Science and Government Report* 30 (June 15, 2000): 1ff.

Interview with Collins discusses the rivalry with Celera, possible positive and negative implications of the sequencing of the human genome, and future research arising from Human Genome Project data.

Office of the Press Secretary. "Remarks by the President, Prime Minister Tony Blair of England (via satellite), Dr. Francis Collins, Director of the National Human Genome Research Institute, and Dr. Craig Venter, President and Chief Scientific Officer, Celera Genomics Corporation, on the Completion of the First Survey of the Entire Human Genome Project." *M2 Presswire*, 30 June 2000, n.p.

Text of the speeches given during the announcement of the Human Genome Project's completion of a rough draft of the human genome on June 26, 2000.

O'Neill, Lucinda M. "An Interview with Francis Collins, MD, Ph.D., Director of the Human Genome Project," *The Exceptional Parent* 32 (October 2002): 28–31.

Collins discusses the implications of the project, particularly for parents.

Selim, Jocelyn, and David Ewing Duncan. "Gene Savant Sifts Life from Seas," *Discover*, December 2004, pp. 18–19.

Short interview with Craig Venter, focusing on his project to sample microbial life in the world's oceans.

Stevens, Tim. "Authors of the Book of Life," *Industry Week,* 11 December 2000, p. 47.
Good overview of the Human Genome Project, including the personalities and rivalry of Francis Collins and Craig Venter.

"Venter, J. Craig." *Current Biography Yearbook 1995,* 573–577. New York: H. W. Wilson, 1995.
Profile of Venter up through his days at TIGR, including quotes from interviews.

Wadman, Meredith. "Biology's Bad Boy Is Back," *Fortune,* 8 March 2004, p. 166ff.
Profile of Craig Venter includes description of his career after the genome project race, with a focus on his attempt to create a synthetic life-form.

Wilkie, Dana. "Ardent Scientist, Savvy Advocate," *The Scientist,* 3 September 2001, p. 1ff.
Short biographical profile and interview with Francis Collins.

Web Sites

National Human Genome Research Institute (NHGRI). This institute, part of the National Institutes of Health, oversees the Human Genome Project and related research. Its Web site has a variety of resources related to the project. For example, its Policy and Ethics section has material on privacy of genetic information, genetic discrimination in employment and insurance, commercialization and patenting, DNA identification in court cases, and genetics and the law. http://www.genome.gov. The project's Ethical, Legal, and Social Implications (ELSI) Research Program has its own page at http://www.genome.gov/10001618. Accessed on December 28, 2004.

CHRONOLOGY

1859	Charles Darwin's *On the Origin of Species* published
1866	Gregor Mendel's paper describing rules of trait inheritance published
1900	Three scientists independently rediscover Mendel's work
1906	William Bateson coins the term *genetics*
1910	Thomas Hunt Morgan's laboratory proves that genes are carried on chromosomes in the nucleus of cells
1944	Oswald Avery shows that bacteria's inherited traits can be changed by exposing them to pure DNA, providing strong evidence that DNA molecules carry inherited information
1952	Robert Briggs and Thomas King clone frogs by somatic cell nuclear transfer, the technique that will later be used to clone mammals
1953	James Watson and Francis Crick's paper describing the structure of DNA molecules published in the April 25 issue of *Nature*
	On May 30, *Nature* publishes second paper by Watson and Crick, in which they propose a mechanism by which a DNA molecule can make a copy of itself
1955	Crick and Sydney Brenner propose that the sequence of bases in DNA encodes information needed for making proteins and that each "letter" of the code is a group of three bases in a certain sequence, or order
	Crick and Brenner suggest a mechanism by which DNA controls the making of proteins through an intermediate molecule, RNA

1960	Ernest McCulloch and James Till identify blood-forming stem cells in adult mice
1961–1965	Marshall Nirenberg and others determine the meanings of the 64 "letters" in the genetic code
1973	Herbert Boyer and Stanley N. Cohen create recombinant DNA and show that it can make proteins when inserted into bacteria, thereby inventing genetic engineering
1975	140 molecular biologists meet in Asilomar, California, on February 24–27, to work out safety guidelines for recombinant DNA experiments
1976	National Institutes of Health draws up safety standards for recombinant DNA research and establish the Recombinant DNA Advisory Committee to evaluate proposed experiments
	Herbert Boyer and Robert Swanson found Genentech, the first business based on genetic engineering technology
	Michael Bishop and Harold Varmus find normal cell gene that resembles a cancer-causing gene (oncogene) and theorize that oncogenes originate in cells rather than in viruses
1980s	Late in the decade, Bert Vogelstein shows that at least four different mutations are required to cause colon cancer
1980	First genetically engineered mammals (mice) produced
	U.S. Supreme Court rules that living things can be patented if human beings have altered them
1981	Robert Weinberg finds first oncogene in a human cancer
	Martin Evans and Matthew Kaufman isolate stem cells from mouse embryos and make them multiply in laboratory dishes
1982	Genentech's recombinant human insulin goes on sale
	First genetically engineered plants are created
1984	Huntington's Disease Collaborative Research Group uses markers (RFLPs) to determine that the Huntington's gene is near the end of the short arm of chromosome 4

1986	Stephen Friend identifies Rb, the first known tumor suppressor gene
1987	In the spring, Steven Lindow conducts tests involving first release of genetically modified organisms (bacteria) into the environment
1989	Human Genome Project begins, with James Watson as director
	Teams led by Francis Collins and Lap-Chee Tsui identify the gene that causes cystic fibrosis
	On May 22, Steven Rosenberg inserts foreign genes into human beings for the first time
1990	Craig Venter and Mark Adams invent expressed sequence tag technique, which speeds up location of genes
	On September 14, French Anderson's group gives Ashanthi DeSilva the first approved gene therapy treatment
1993	Nancy Wexler and others identify gene that causes Huntington's disease
	Cynthia Kenyon shows that changes in two genes make nematode worms live twice as long as normal
	Francis Collins takes over leadership of Human Genome Project
1995	Craig Venter's laboratory sequences first genome of a living thing (a bacterium)
	In July, Ian Wilmut's laboratory produces cloned sheep from cultured cells
	In August, James Thomson announces the isolation of embryonic stem cells from monkeys
1996	Dolly, sheep cloned from a mature adult cell by Ian Wilmut's laboratory, is born on July 5
1997	First newspaper story about Dolly appears on February 22
	In July, Ian Wilmut's group announces the birth of Polly, a sheep that is both cloned and genetically altered
1998	In May, Craig Venter's Celera Genomic Corporation claims that it will sequence the human genome sooner and at less cost than the Human Genome Project

On November 26, James Thomson publishes article stating that his laboratory has grown human embryonic stem cells in culture for five months

1999   In August, Ingo Potrykus announces creation of golden rice, which has been genetically altered to contain a precursor of vitamin A and could therefore treat or prevent vitamin A deficiency in developing countries

Jesse Gelsinger dies as a result of a gene therapy treatment in September

2000   Accompanied by Francis Collins and Craig Venter, President Bill Clinton announces completion of a rough draft of the sequence of the human genome on June 26

2001   President George W. Bush rules on August 9 that federal funding may support research on existing human embryonic stem cell lines but not research involving creation of new cell lines

2002   Early in the year, two groups of scientists extend the lives of mice by altering genes similar to those discovered in worms by Cynthia Kenyon

2003   Cynthia Kenyon produces worms that live six times as long as normal and remain healthy and active for most of that time

On April 25, the 50th anniversary of the publication of Watson and Crick's paper describing the structure of DNA, Human Genome Project scientists announce completion of the final version of the sequence of the human genome

GLOSSARY

acceptor molecule   early name for what was later called transfer RNA

ADA deficiency   rare inherited illness caused by lack of the gene that makes adenosine deaminase, resulting in a nonfunctioning immune system and great susceptibility to infections

adenine   one of the four kinds of bases in nucleic acid (DNA and RNA) molecules

adenosine deaminase (ADA)   a protein required by some cells in the immune system; without it, the immune system cannot function

adult stem cells   long-lived cells found in various tissues that can make a number of different cell types, but not as many types as embryonic stem cells can make; stem cells from living things in any stage of development later than the embryo, even fetuses, are considered adult

Agrobacterium tumefaciens   a species of bacteria that infects plants, causing tumorlike growths (galls); genetic engineers sometimes use it to add genes to plant genomes

AIDS (acquired immunodeficiency syndrome)   an illness that destroys the immune system; most scientists believe that it is caused by HIV, a retrovirus

Alzheimer's disease   a disease of unknown cause, diagnosed most often in old people, that destroys the brain, causing memory loss and confusion (dementia)

amino acid   One of 20 types of compounds that combine to form protein molecules

amyotrophic lateral sclerosis (ALS)   a disease of unknown cause that destroys peripheral nerves, causing increasing paralysis and eventual death; also called Lou Gehrig's disease or (in Britain) motor neurone disease

181

artificial insemination creation of a pregnancy by artificially inserting sperm into the body of a female

base one of four types of chemical subunits in a nucleic acid (DNA or RNA) molecule; the bases in DNA are adenine, cytosine, guanine, and thymine

beta-carotene a yellowish pigment, found in some plants, that is a precursor of vitamin A

biotechnology any technology that makes use of living organisms; today, often used to mean technology that makes use of genetically modified organisms

blastocyst an early stage of embryonic development in which the embryo consists of a hollow ball of about 200 cells

bone marrow the fatty material inside most bones; it contains adult stem cells that make all the cells in the blood

Caenorhabditis elegans a species of nematode, or roundworm, frequently used for genetic experiments, including experiments related to aging

carbohydrates a class of foods containing carbon, hydrogen, and oxygen; sugars and starches, such as pasta, rice, and potatoes

carcinogen a factor, especially a chemical, that can cause cancer

carrier a healthy person who has inherited a single copy of a defective gene and can pass that gene on to offspring

cell cycle the cycle of resting and growth, resulting in cell division, through which cells pass repeatedly

cell line a colony of cells developed in a laboratory from a single original cell

chimera an organism whose body includes two or more types of cells containing different sets of genes

chromosomes threadlike bodies, made of protein and DNA, found in the nucleus of cells; they are arranged in pairs (23 pairs in humans) and carry inherited information (genes)

clone an organism that has exactly the same genes as another organism

colon the lowest part of the large intestine

conditional tumor suppressor gene a class of gene that can either cause or prevent cancer, depending on its interaction with a certain protein

conjugation a sexlike process through which bacteria or other simple organisms exchange genetic information

culture growth of microorganisms or plant or animal cells in a nourishing fluid or solid in a laboratory

cystic fibrosis an inherited disease that, among other things, causes the formation of thick mucus and makes the lungs susceptible to damaging infections

cytoplasm the jellylike material that makes up the body of a cell

cytosine one of the four types of bases in nucleic acid (DNA and RNA) molecules

daf-2, daf-16 two genes in the roundworm *Caenorhabditis elegans* that help determine how long the worm will live

deoxyribonucleic acid (DNA) the complex substance that carries inherited information in most organisms

diabetes a severe illness caused by destruction of cells that make the hormone insulin (type 1 diabetes) or by the body becoming resistant to the action of insulin (type 2 diabetes)

differentiated cell a cell that has matured into a particular type, such as a muscle cell or nerve cell

dominant gene a gene that produces a particular protein, effect, or trait even if an organism inherits only one copy of that gene

embryo an organism in an early stage of development before birth; in humans, an unborn child is considered to be an embryo during the first seven weeks of development

embryology the scientific study of the way living things develop before birth

embryonic stem cells cells found inside the blastocyst of an embryo that can form almost any cell type in the body

endosperm the tissue that surrounds the developing embryo in a plant seed and provides nourishment for the embryo's growth

enzyme a protein that starts or greatly speeds up a chemical reaction

epidermis the outermost layer of the skin

Escherichia coli (E. coli) a common and usually harmless species of bacteria that lives in the human intestine; it has often been used in genetics and genetic engineering experiments

evolution by natural selection theory developed by 19th-century biologist Charles Darwin, stating that species become better adapted to their environment over time because only characteristics that help members of the species survive and reproduce in a particular environment will be passed on through multiple generations

expressed sequence tags small segments from portions of DNA that are active (expressed) in a cell; when sequenced, they can be used to isolate previously unknown genes

fetus an unborn vertebrate animal in a relatively late stage of development (after seven weeks in a human)

free radicals atoms or molecules with unpaired electrons, which makes them highly likely to take part in chemical reactions; such compounds are likely to cause damage in cells

fungus one of a group of organisms, including molds and mushrooms, that reproduce by spores and either are parasites on living organisms or consume dead matter

gene a specific part of a nucleic acid molecule that acts as a unit of inherited information; it may determine a characteristic (trait), make one or more proteins, or affect the action of other genes

gene amplification a process in which abnormal extra copies of a gene are produced, resulting in an increase in the making of a protein or other activity carried out by the gene

gene enhancement altering genes in order to produce improvements, such as increased strength or intelligence, in a basically healthy organism

gene therapy altering genes in order to prevent or cure disease

genetic engineering altering genes or DNA directly through recombination, rather than through breeding

genetics the branch of science that studies inheritance of traits and variation in related organisms

genome an organism's complete collection of genes or genetic material

germ cells precursors of sex cells

germ-line genes genes that are contained in sex cells and therefore can be passed on to offspring

glutamine an amino acid that plays various roles in the nervous system and sometimes damages nerve cells

GMOs genetically modified organisms

graft tissue transplanted from another site on the body or from another organism

guanine one of the four types of bases in nucleic acid (DNA and RNA) molecules

helix a spiral or corkscrew shape; a DNA molecule is a helix

hemoglobin the iron-containing pigment that gives blood its red color and allows certain cells in the blood to carry oxygen

hemophilia an inherited disease in which the absence of substances needed to make the blood clot results in dangerously excessive bleeding from even slight injuries

hepatitis B a serious liver disease caused by a virus

HIV (human immunodeficiency virus) the retrovirus usually considered to be the cause of AIDS

hormone a protein made in one part of the body that is carried to other parts of the body and affects cells there

HTLV (human T-cell leukemia virus) a retrovirus that causes a form of leukemia

Human Genome Project a giant international project, begun in the United States in 1989, whose goal was to determine the sequence of bases in the entire human genome

human growth hormone a protein made in the pituitary gland that directs normal growth in young people and may help maintain health throughout life

huntingtin the protein made by the gene which, in abnormal form, causes Huntington's disease; the protein's exact function is unknown, but it may affect the way cells use energy

Huntington's disease an inherited disease, caused by a dominant gene, that causes progressive brain damage, resulting in writhing movements, memory loss, and confusion (dementia)

ice-minus bacteria mutated form of *Pseudomonas syringae* bacteria lacking the gene that makes the normal form of the bacteria help form ice crystals on plants

immune system the system consisting of several types of cells and body fluids that detects and destroys microorganisms and other foreign materials that could cause disease

in vitro fertilization joining of sperm and egg in a laboratory dish or other artificial container

infectious disease   a disease caused by microorganisms or other parasites

insulin   a hormone produced by certain cells in the pancreas that affects the way the body uses foods, particularly sugars and other carbohydrates

"junk DNA"   DNA of unknown function that lies between genes; also called introns

leukemia   a cancer of white blood cells

ligase   one of a group of enzymes that can attach pieces of DNA to one another

malaria   a serious blood disease caused by a microscopic parasite

melanoma   a fast-growing, deadly skin cancer

messenger RNA   a single-stranded copy of segments of DNA that travels from the nucleus to the cytoplasm and provides instructions for the making of protein molecules

molecular biology   the branch of science that studies the physical and chemical properties and activities of molecules within living cells

moratorium   a temporary halt to an activity

mutation   a change in a gene

National Institutes of Health (NIH)   a group of large research institutions in Bethesda, Maryland, supported by the U.S. government

nematode   a type of worm with a long, cylindrical, unsegmented body; also called a roundworm

nucleic acid   complex organic acids found in all living cells; the two types of nucleic acids are RNA (ribonucleic acid) and DNA (deoxyribonucleic acid)

nucleus   a central body found in most cells, which contains the material that carries inherited information

obesity   the medical condition of being extremely overweight

oncogene   a type of gene that, when activated, causes cancer

organochlorines   chemicals found in pesticides, plastics, and many other common materials; they appear to affect the actions of hormones in living bodies and may cause illness or abnormal development in animals and humans

p53   a tumor suppressor gene that is inactivated in many kinds of cancer

pancreas an organ in the abdomen that produces substances that help digestion in the small intestine; certain cells in the pancreas also make the hormone insulin

parasite an organism that takes its nourishment from another living organism

PEG-ADA a combination of polyethylene glycol (PEG) and adenosine deaminase (ADA) that can survive in the blood and is used to treat people with ADA deficiency

Penicillium one of a genus (group of related species) of greenish molds that grow on bread, cheese, and other materials; the antibiotic penicillin comes from some species

petri dish a shallow, round, transparent glass or plastic dish used in laboratories to contain colonies of microorganisms or cells

pharming genetically altering plants or animals so that they will produce drugs

plasmid a small, circular piece of DNA found in some bacteria; it is separate from a bacterium's main genome and can transfer genetic information between bacteria either naturally or artificially

polio (poliomyelitis) a disease caused by a virus that can cause paralysis and muscle wasting

positional cloning a technique invented by Francis Collins that allows researchers looking for disease-causing genes to move along a chromosome in "jumps" rather than base by base, thus speeding the search

preexisting condition a medical condition that a person suffers from or has suffered from at the time he or she takes out a health insurance policy; such conditions are often excluded from the policy's coverage

primate any one of an order of mammals possessing flexible hands and feet with five digits, including humans, great apes, and monkeys

promoter a stretch of DNA next to a gene that activates the gene

protein one of a large group of biological chemicals consisting of long chains of amino acids; proteins are found in all cells and do most of the work in the cells

Pseudomonas syringae a species of bacteria, extremely common in the air of natural environments, possessing a protein on its surface that causes ice crystals to form at a higher temperature than they would otherwise

ras an oncogene (cancer-causing gene) first found in virus-caused rat sarcomas; it was the first oncogene to be identified in a human cancer

Rb the first tumor suppressor gene to be discovered; it was first found in retinoblastoma, a cancer of the human eye, but was later detected in several other types of human cancer as well

receptor a protein on the surface of cells that binds to a particular hormone or other substance coming from outside the cell; this binding triggers a chain of chemical activity in the cell

recessive gene a gene that produces a protein, effect, or trait only when an organism inherits identical copies of the gene from both parents

recombinant DNA a DNA molecule made from segments of DNA taken from two different organisms (often two different species of organisms) and combined in the laboratory

Recombinant DNA Advisory Committee (RAC) a committee established by the National Institutes of Health in 1986 to evaluate the safety of recombinant DNA experiments; today it chiefly evaluates tests that involve giving altered genes to human beings

regeneration growing back an organ or body part lost to injury or disease

reproductive cloning cloning done with the aim of producing a fully developed organism, such as a human baby

restriction enzyme one of a group of enzymes made by certain bacteria, whose natural purpose is to halt virus infections by cutting apart the virus's DNA; geneticists and genetic engineers use these enzymes to divide DNA molecules into segments with predictable beginning and ending sequences

retinoblastoma a rare cancer of the human eye that is sometimes inherited and sometimes arises spontaneously; the first known tumor suppressor gene was isolated from this type of cancer

retrovirus one of a group of viruses that carry their genetic material in RNA rather than DNA; they can make a DNA copy of this material and insert it into the genome of cells they infect, causing their genes to be copied when the cells reproduce their own genomes

restriction fragment length polymorphism (RFLP) a stretch of a DNA molecule that can be inherited in a number of different forms, producing fragments of different lengths when the molecule is treated with a restriction enzyme; RFLPs can be used as markers to help researchers locate genes

ribosome   a body within a cell that creates proteins by assembling amino acids in a sequence specified by the sequence of bases in messenger RNA

ribonucleic acid (RNA)   a nucleic acid that contains uracil instead of thymine as a base (its other three types of bases are the same as in DNA); it serves primarily as a messenger chemical, conveying DNA instructions from the nucleus to other parts of the cell

roundworm   one of a group of worms with long, cylindrical, unsegmented bodies; also called nematodes

Rous sarcoma virus   a virus that causes a type of cancer in chickens; its existence was first predicted by Francis Peyton Rous in 1910

sarcoma   a type of cancerous tumor that begins in connective tissue or muscle

sequence   the order in which members of a group appear; the genetic code is specified through the sequence of bases in a DNA or RNA molecule

sequencing   determining or identifying the sequence of bases within a DNA molecule

sex cells   the cells (sperm from males and eggs from females) that combine to produce a new organism and carry genes from the parents into that organism

sickle-cell anemia   an inherited disease in which hemoglobin, and the shape of the red blood cells that carry that hemoglobin, are abnormal

side effects   unintended and usually undesirable effects of a drug or other medical treatment

smallpox   a disfiguring and often fatal illness caused by the variola virus

somatic cell nuclear transfer   a method of cloning that involves removing the nucleus from an egg cell and combining the cell with a body cell containing a nucleus

src   an oncogene first detected in chicken tumors caused by the Rous sarcoma virus; it was shown to have come from normal chicken cells

staphylococcus   one of a common group of bacterial species that cause serious wound infections

stem cells undifferentiated cells that can give rise to a wide variety of differentiated cell types

SV40 (simian virus 40) a virus that infects monkeys and can cause cancer in some kinds of animals

teratoma (teratocarcinoma) a cancerous tumor, arising from a single germ cell, that contains many types of differentiated cells in a disorganized mass

"test-tube baby" a child created by in vitro fertilization

thalassemia an inherited blood disease in which the blood contains an abnormal form of hemoglobin; it is chiefly found in people whose ancestors came from the Mediterranean Sea area

therapeutic cloning cloning for research or medical purposes, usually to create embryos from which embryonic stem cells can be harvested; the clones are not allowed to develop into complete organisms

thymine one of the four kinds of bases in a DNA molecule

trait a specific characteristic of a living thing, often one determined by heredity (genes)

transfer RNA a small RNA molecule, formerly called an adapter molecule, that attaches a particular type of amino acid to a protein being assembled in a cell

transgenic organism an organism containing a gene or DNA sequence, in all its cells, that comes from a genetically different organism, often a different species

tumor suppressor gene a type of gene that, when made inactive by mutation, produces cancer

umbilical cord the rope of blood vessels that binds a baby to its mother before birth and conveys nourishment from the mother

uracil the type of base in RNA that takes the place of thymine in DNA

vector a living thing that carries or transmits something, such as a gene or a disease-causing microorganism, into another living thing

virus a being consisting of protein and nucleic acid that is considered to be on the border between living and nonliving things; it can reproduce only by infecting cells

vitamin A a substance contained in foods such as green leafy vegetables that is necessary for healthy skin, eyes, and immune system

white cell   one of several types of blood cells that play roles in the body's immune system

whole genome shotgun sequencing   a rapid genome sequencing technique, invented by Craig Venter, in which an organism's genome is broken up into many small fragments, which are then sequenced and reassembled in order by a computer

X-ray crystallography   a technique that uses beams of X-rays shot through a crystal or other solid to determine the three-dimensional layout of atoms within the molecules of the solid

Y chromosome   a small chromosome found only in males

zygote   a fertilized egg cell, formed by the union of a sperm and an unfertilized egg; the zygote is capable of producing a complete offspring organism

FURTHER RESOURCES

Books

Cherfas, Jeremy, ed. *Essential Science: The Human Genome.* London: DK Books, 2002.
  Explains the Human Genome Project and its implications for a nonscientific audience, using lively text and many graphics.
Conley, Beverly D. *Biological Revolution.* Philadelphia: Xlibris Corp., 2002.
  Reviews biotechnology and related scientific developments, highlighting moral, legal, and ethical questions they raise.
DeSalle, Rob, and Michael Yudell. *Welcome to the Genome.* Hoboken, N.J.: Wiley, 2004.
  Well-illustrated book describes recent research on the human genome and the controversial issues it brings up.
Howard Hughes Medical Institute. *Exploring the Biomedical Revolution.* Baltimore, Md.: Johns Hopkins University Press, 2000.
  Leading science writers tell the human stories behind 20th-century medical advances, including those related to genetics, from both the researchers' and the patients' points of view. Includes fold-out charts and a stereoscopic viewer that reveals 3-D images.
Reilly, Philip R. *Abraham Lincoln's DNA and Other Adventures in Genetics.* Cold Spring Harbor, N.Y.: Cold Spring Harbor Laboratory Press, 2000.
  Wide-ranging tales of crime, history, and human behavior illustrate the principles of human genetics and issues that genetic science raises.
Ridley, Matt. *Genome.* New York: HarperCollins, 2000.
  This book's 23 chapters, one for each of a human's pair of chromosomes, provide a "whistle-stop tour" of the human genome. The author uses the story of a gene from each chromosome to convey considerable information about genetic science and human development in an entertaining way.
Schachter, Bernice. *Issues and Dilemmas of Biotechnology: A Reference Guide.* Westport, Conn.: Greenwood Publishing Group, 2000.

A reference for advanced high school students and teachers that provides background on the science of biotechnology and the views of different groups about controversial issues such as genetically modified food, the patenting of human genes, genetic testing, and cloning.

Smith, Gina. *The Genomics Age.* New York: AMACOM Books, 2004.
Describes how discoveries about the human genome are changing, or are likely to change, society and people's understanding of humanity.

Steinberg, Mark L., and Sharon D. Cosloy. *The Facts on File Dictionary of Biotechnology and Genetic Engineering.* New York: Facts On File, 2000.
About 2,000 entries, illustrated with drawings.

Torr, James D., ed. *Genetic Engineering: Opposing Viewpoints.* San Diego, Calif.: Greenhaven Press, 2000.
Anthology of articles expressing various viewpoints on questions such as how genetic engineering will affect society and how it should be regulated.

Watson, James D., with Andrew Berry. *DNA: The Secret of Life.* New York: Alfred A. Knopf, 2003.
History of modern genetics and genetic engineering, including discussion of social implications.

Witherly, Jeffre, Galen P. Perry, and Daryl L. Leja. *An A to Z of DNA Science: What Scientists Mean When They Talk about Genes and Genomes.* Cold Spring Harbor, N.Y.: Cold Spring Harbor Laboratory Press, 2001.
Defines and illustrates more than 200 specialized terms in ways that nonspecialists can understand.

Internet Resources

About Biotech. Access Excellence. Available online. URL: http://www.access excellence.org/RC. Accessed on May 4, 2006.
This site is designed for biology teachers and students. Subsections include Issues and Ethics, Biotech Applied, and Biotech Chronicles (history).

AgBioTech InfoNet. Available online. URL: http://www.biotech-info.net. Accessed on May 4, 2006.
Extensive site about applications of genetic engineering to agriculture and the effects and implications of the technology presents papers both favoring and criticizing agricultural genetic engineering.

BioTech: Life Science Resources and Reference Tools. Indiana University and University of Texas. Available online. URL: http://biotech.icmb.utexas. edu. Accessed on May 4, 2006.
Site includes an illustrated dictionary, an extensive list of science resource links, and BioMedLink, a large database of biomedical sites.

Foundations of Classical Genetics. Electronic Scholarly Publishing. Available online. URL: http://www.esp.org/foundations/genetics/classical. Accessed on May 4, 2006.

Offers digitized versions of original manuscripts of Gregor Mendel's paper on pea plant inheritance and other important papers in the history of genetics research. It also has a chronology and links to related sites.

Genetic Education Center. University of Kansas Medical Center. Available online. URL: http://www.kumc.edu/gec. Accessed on May 4, 2006.

Designed for educators interested in the Human Genome Project and human genetics, this site includes lesson plans, educational resources and activities, glossaries, extensive links, and more.

GeneWatch UK. Available online. URL: http://www.genewatch.org. Accessed on May 4, 2006.

Site of British organization that is generally negative toward genetic modification provides access to a wide variety of news stories and reports on the subject. Topics covered include genetically modified crops and foods, genetically modified animals, human genetics, laboratory use of genetics, biological weapons, and patenting of genes and living things.

National Center for Biotechnology Information. National Library of Medicine and National Institutes of Health. Available online. URL: http://www.ncbi.nlm.nih.gov. Accessed on May 4, 2006.

Provides access to a variety of human genome and other gene sequence databases, as well as to PubMed Central, a free archive of life science journals.

National Human Genome Research Institute (NHGRI). Available online. URL: http://www.genome.gov. Accessed on May 4, 2006.

Site of the institute that led the Human Genome Project for the National Institutes of Health includes news, current research, educational resources, and discussions of policy and ethics.

Omics Gateway. *Nature* magazine. Available online. URL: http://www.nature.com/omics/index.html. Accessed on May 4, 2006.

Includes links to news; original research papers, information about genomics, proteomics, and related subjects; and new applications of sequencing research and technologies.

The Institute for Genomic Research (TIGR). Available online. URL: http://www.tigr.org. Accessed on May 4, 2006.

Site links to news, organizations, genome maps and sequences for various organisms, and more.

Periodicals

Discover
Published by the Walt Disney Company
114 Fifth Avenue
New York, NY 10011
Telephone: (212) 633-4400
www.discover.com
  A popular monthly magazine containing articles on a variety of science topics, including genetics and genetic engineering.

Genetic Engineering News
Published by BD Biosciences
2 Madison Avenue
Larchmont, NY 10538
Telephone: (914) 834-3880
www.genengnews.com
  Business-oriented weekly magazine describes advances in biotechnology and genetic engineering.

Nature
Published by Nature Publishing Group
968 National Press Building
529 14th Street, NW
Washington, DC 20045-1938
Telephone: (202) 737-2355
www.nature.com
  A prestigious source of scientific papers, originally published in Europe.

Science
Published by the American Association for the Advancement of Science
1200 New York Avenue, NW
Washington, DC 20005
Telephone: (202) 326-6400
www.sciencemag.org
  Prestigious American source of scientific papers.

Science News
Published by Science Service
1719 N Street, NW
Washington, DC 20036
Telephone: (202) 785-2255
www.sciencenews.org
 Weekly newsletter contains brief descriptions of current scientific advances.

Scientific American
415 Madison Avenue
New York, NY 10017
Telephone: (212) 754-0550
www.sciam.com
 Monthly magazine publishing lengthy articles on a wide range of scientific subjects. More difficult reading than *Discover,* less difficult than *Science* or *Nature.*

Societies and Organizations

American Genetic Association (www.theaga.org/overview.html) P.O. Box 257, Buckeystown, MD 21717-0257. Telephone: (301) 695-9292.

Biotechnology Industry Organization (www.bio.org) 1225 I Street, NW, Suite 400, Washington, DC 2005. Telephone: (202) 962-9200.

Foundation on Economic Trends (www.foet.org) 4520 East West Highway, Suite 600, Bethseda, MD 20814. Telephone: (301) 656-6272.

Genetics Society of America (www.genetics-gsa.org) 9650 Rockville Pike, Bethesda, MD 20814-3998. Telephone: (301) 634-7300.

Office of Biotechnology Activities, National Institutes of Health (www4. od.nih.gov/oba) 6705 Rockledge Drive, Suite 750, MSC 7985, Bethesda, MD 20892-7985. Telephone: (301) 496-9838.

Pew Initiative on Food and Biotechnology (http://pewagbiotech.org) 1331 H Street, NW, Suite 900, Washington, DC 20005. Telephone: (202) 347-9044.

INDEX

Note: *Italic* page numbers indicate illustrations.

A

Academy of Achievement 107
Academy of Sciences (France) 10
ADA deficiency 59–61, 63–65, 67
Adams, Mark 165
adapter molecules 14, 27
adenine 3, 7–9, *9*, 84
adenosine deaminase (ADA) 60–61, 64–67
AgBioView 142–143, 145, 152
aging
  genes and xix, 91–93, 95–105
  stem cells to prevent 127
Agrobacterium tumefaciens 143, *144*
AIDS 41, 60, 67
Albany Medical Center Prize 33
Alexander Fleming: The Man and the Myth (Macfarlane) 95
Alexandra (czarina of Russia) 76
Alexis (crown prince of Russia) 76
Altered Fates (Lyon, Gorner) 57
Alzheimer's disease 101, 102, 132
American Academy of Achievement 135
American Health 73
American Society of Gene Therapy 69

American Society of Plant Biologists 153
Amherst College 39
amino acids 1, 10, *13*, 14, 27, 84
amyotrophic lateral sclerosis (ALS) 118
Anderson, Kathy 60, 69
Anderson, W. French xix, 27, 56–72, *57, 65*
  awards 70
  chronology 70–71
  further reading 71–72
  invents gene therapy 56, 58, 60–61, 63–65
  later years 67, 69
  youth and education 56–58
Angier, Natalie 39, 51
Animal Breeding Research Station 108
Annunzio, Frank, Award 136
Antinori, Severino 117
Applied Biosystems 167
Asilomar conference 28–29, 32
Astbury, W. T. 6
AstraZeneca 150–151
Avastin 33
Avery, Oswald 2

B

bacteria 92, 94, 95, 99, 108, 143, 165
  as genetically engineered "factories" 22, 30, 31, 109
  DNA affecting 2
  "ice-minus" 148
  in first genetic engineering experiments 23, 24, 25

plasmids in 22, 24
restriction enzymes in 21, 23
synthetic 169–170
Baltimore, David 51
Basel, University of 140
bases in nucleic acid molecules 1, 3, 6–9, *9*, *11*, 21
  sequence of 21–22
  as genetic code 10, 13
  technology for determining 159, 163–168
Bateson, William xvii
Berg, Paul 26–27, 32
Bernal, J. Desmond 6, 12
beta-carotene 142–144, 147, 153
Beyer, Peter 142–145, 150–151, 153
biotechnology industry
  agricultural xix, 139, 145–157
  animal 108–109
  plant 145–157
  criticisms of 109, 139–140, 145–149, 151–152
  expansion 33, 145–146
  modern, origin of xvi, 29–33
  patenting of living things in 150–152
  praise for 147, 149
Birkbeck College 12
birth, development before 94, 107, 123, 135
Bishop, Michael xviii, 38–40, *42*, 42–43, 45–46, 49–55
  awards 49–50
  chronology 51–53

197

V

Varmus, Harold xviii,
38–40, 39, 42–43, 45–46,
49–55, 132
  awards 49–51
  chronology 51–53
  codiscovers cellular
    oncogenes 42–43, 45,
    46, 51
  further reading 53–55
  later years 49
  youth and education 39
Vest, Charles M. 34
Venter, Craig xx, 159,
162–176, 163
  awards 169
  chronology 172–174
  further reading 174–176
  Human Genome Project,
    evaluation of 170–171
  improves sequencing
    technology 164–166,
    168
  leadership skills 166–
    167
  recent projects 169–170
  sequences human genome
    163, 168–169
  youth and education
    164
Victoria, Queen 76
Virginia, University of 161
viruses 4, 21, 49
  as gene carriers 58, 64,
    67, 69, 143
  cancer-causing xviii, 26,
    40–45
  genetic engineering of
    26, 28
  RNA 41
  structure 12
vitamin A deficiency 139,
  141, 142, 147, 149
Vogelstein, Bert 48

W

Wadman, Meredith 165
Washington, University of
  (Seattle) 85

Washington University (St.
  Louis) 27
Watson, James xviii, 2,
3–19, 40, 58, 66, 92
  awards 10
  chronology 16–17
  codiscovers DNA struc-
    ture 5–10, 12, 15, 27,
    56, 57, 171
  codiscovers how DNA
    reproduces 7–8, 10, 27
  further reading 18–19
  later years 14–15
  leads Human Genome
    Project 15, 160–161
  youth and education 3–4
Weinberg, Robert 43–44,
  46, 48
West, Michael 127
Wexler, Alice 73
Wexler, Leonore 73–75
Wexler, Milton 73–75
Wexler, Nancy xix, 73–90,
  74, 86, 162
  awards 87
  chronology 87–88
  coordinates search for
    Huntington's gene 84
  discrimination, genetic,
    views on 83
  further reading 89–90
  learns about mother's ill-
    ness 73–74
  recent research 85–87
  studies Venezuelan family
    with Huntington's dis-
    ease 78–80, 85–87
  youth and education,
    73, 75
W. French Anderson: Father
  of Gene Therapy (Burke,
  Epperson) 69
What Is Life? (Schrödinger)
  4
What Mad Pursuit (Crick) 4
white cells 60, 63–65, 67
Whitehead Institute 43
whole genome shotgun
  sequencing 165, 168, 170

WiCell Rresearch Institute
  135
Wilkie, Dana 162
Wilkins, Maurice 3–5, 10,
  12
Willadsen, Steen 111–112
Wilmut, Ian xix, 106–121,
  107, 116, 132, 149
  animal cloning experi-
    ments 110–114, 131
  awards 118
  chronology 119–120
  early career 108
  further reading 120–121
  human cloning for stem
    cell research 118, 133
  youth and education
    106–108
Wilson, Edward O. 102
Wisconsin, University of
  122, 126, 128–129, 132,
  135–136
Wisconsin Alumni Research
  Foundation (WARF) 129,
  134, 135
Wizard of Oz, The 161
World Health Organization
  142
Wyngaarden, James 160

X

X-ray crystallography 3–4,
  6, 8, 12
X-rays 42–43

Y

Yale University 21, 161–162
Y chromosome xvii
Ye, Xudong 143, 146
Yunis, Jorge 46

Z

Zeneca 150–151